Make Sh** Happen

Unclutter Your Life

Deborah LeBlanc, CCHt, CAHA

Copyright © 2024 Deborah LeBlanc, CCHt, CAHA

All rights reserved.

The contents of this book may not be reproduced, duplicated, or transmitted without direct written permission from the author.

Under no circumstances will any legal responsibility or blame be held against the publisher for any reparation, damages, or monetary loss due to the information herein, either directly or indirectly.

Legal Notice:

This book is copyright-protected. This is only for personal use. You cannot amend, distribute, sell, use, quote, or paraphrase any part of the content within this book without the consent of the author.

Disclaimer Notice:

Please note the information contained within this document is for educational and entertainment purposes only. Every attempt has been made to provide accurate, up-to-date, reliable, and complete information. No warranties of any kind are expressed or implied. Readers acknowledge that the author is not engaging in the rendering of legal, financial, medical, or professional advice. The content of this book has been derived from various sources. Please consult a licensed professional before attempting any techniques outlined in this book.

By reading this document, the reader agrees that under no circumstances is the author responsible for any losses, direct or indirect, which are incurred as a result of the use of the information contained within this document, including, but not limited to, errors, omissions, or inaccuracies.

Contents

Introduction	4
1. Different Kinds of Clutter	9
2. Make an Actual Plan	24
3. Stop Making Excuses	32
4. Declutter Your House	41
5. Declutter at Work	55
6. Declutter Your Mind and Habits	61
7. Keep Your Sh** Decluttered	71
8. Level Up!	81
9. Simple Doesn't Mean Basic	93
Conclusion	105
Additional Resources	108

Introduction

Welcome to *Make Sh** Happen: Unclutter Your Life*. If you picked up this book, it's likely that you feel there are areas of your life that need some organizing—be that in your physical house or office, your digital space, your head, or anywhere else. Does that sound like you? If yes...awesome! Thank you so much for taking this step to better yourself and the world around you. We're honored you chose us to help you through this important journey.

Here's what to expect: a no-nonsense (but that's not to say a little fun) guide for those who feel more at peace when physical, environmental, mental, etc. surroundings are uncluttered but haven't found a way to either start the process of removing clutter or haven't found a realistic routine to *keep* things in their place.

This book is for those who look at a mess and say, "I'll do it tomorrow," or who have unpleasant thoughts when they see their messy houses but think, "Eh. I'll just deal with it," and move onto the next thing. There's absolutely no reason for you to continue living that way! You deserve to live in an environment and mental state that serves and works for you, *not* against you. Hopefully after reading this book, you'll understand the difference (if you don't already).

Say, for instance, you really want to declutter your home. Easy! The first step is to get a big trash bag and go from room to room looking for things like knickknacks, expired makeup or food, old tissues, and anything else that is taking up valuable space. (This doesn't include things that can be donated or recycled; those should be put in a separate spot.) Another great trick is to get totes to store your seasonal items (such as heavy blankets used in the fall or winter, large cooking pans that you only pull out for special occasions, decorations, etc.) in your basement or garage. Things that are of limited use can easily turn into clutter!

Another example would be decluttering your computer or phone. Fortunately, this task can also be seen as somewhat simple. We're so lucky to have ways to digitally back files up, so loading old or unhelpful documents onto cloud storage will save you headaches when worrying about the location of files or photos. That way, you can be rest assured that if anything ever happens with your technology—should your devices stop working or get lost—you will always have access to your important files. But please don't just haphazardly load all of the files on your computer. First, delete anything that doesn't serve you anymore.

What if you just want to declutter your life in general? Don't worry! We've got you there too. One of the best gifts you can give yourself is called a "calendar audit." This requires going through your digital or paper calendar each week, month, or however often you feel it necessary, and questioning every event or task. If it doesn't serve you, your career, your friendships, etc., it's probably best to take them off. For example, let's imagine you have a date with someone you really don't feel connected to in the first place, and you're really tired that week. Politely and kindly cancel. By creating more space on your agenda, you'll find that you have more time to do things that you enjoy, like reading, writing, binge-watching the latest Netflix show, whatever.

Setting goals can also help you to organize your life. A way to do this is by starting with the things in life you hope to do or acquire in the future and working backward from there. Like our date example, if you truly want to be married in, let's say, the next five years—ask yourself if going on this bad date will help you get closer to that goal. In all likelihood, probably not. That's not to say he, she, or they are bad people. They just might not be the right person for you. You'll probably find that once you start thinking this way, it will become a habit, and you'll assess every action or decision you make through this lens.

We hope you're starting to see why decluttering your life in all aspects is so important. However, if you need a little more convincing, let's picture this. You are in your ideal profession, making more than enough money to pay the bills, you have the partner and/or family you've always wanted, and you live in your dream home. Ponder what that really looks like. Once you have a clear image, you'll hopefully see that people who work hard to achieve and receive what they want in life do so by being clear and organized regarding their personal surroundings, mental spaces, personal relationships, etc.

No, we aren't saying that only organized people can be successful in life. But we ARE suggesting that it can be easier for organized people to achieve their goals because they have a clearer understanding of exactly what they want in life. Clutter can only obscure or hide that.

It's also important to realize that messes are physically and mentally dangerous. You read that right. Not only are piles of stuff hard to look at, but they can also cause you stress, poor health, and well-being concerns. For example, studies have shown that a poorly organized home can be harder to enter and evacuate by firefighters in the unfortunate event of a fire. And the cases of trips and falls in unorganized spaces are also much higher in cluttered spaces—for what we assume are obvious reasons. Misplaced toys, boxes, etc., may as well be booby traps. Moreover, it has been proven that people with messy houses are sometimes more forgetful and less apathetic, hospitable, and open to others. Not to mention the increase in allergic symptoms in untidy environments for people who suffer from allergies to things like dust and pet dander, which tend to collect in places that are not often cleaned.

It is our sincerest hope that through this book, you'll learn the tools to help you reorganize your life by celebrating the little victories as well as the big ones. Did you take your garbage out to the bin today instead of letting it accumulate in your garage? That's awesome! Did you dust the little whiskers you'd usually leave behind on your bathroom vanity? Great! Did you say no to plans because you feel like they don't align with your overall goals or you'd benefit more from some personal space? Go you! Large changes often come from making little ones throughout the journey. And once you start making conscious efforts to protect your time, your mental health, and the organization of your personal belongings, you probably won't be able to stop. Think of it this way—*keeping* a house, your mind, your calendar, etc., clean and organized is a LOT easier than starting from scratch.

So, crawl into your favorite reading nook, grab a highlighter and pen to take notes, and start the journey of becoming your best and most organized self.

This is your time, your turn, and your book.

"Getting organized is a sign of self-respect."
~ Gabrielle Bernstein

"The only difference between a mob and a trained army is organization."
~ Calvin Coolidge

"It takes as much energy to wish as it does to plan."
~ Eleanor Roosevelt

"Clutter is no more than postponed decisions."
~ Barbara Hemphill

"People cannot change their tidying habits without first changing their way of thinking."
~ Marie Kondo

"Success is the sum of small efforts repeated day in and day out."
~ Robert Collier

Chapter One

Different Kinds of Clutter

> "Simplicity is not the absence of clutter; that's a consequence of simplicity."
>
> ~ Jonathon Ive

Welcome once again to a journey that's all about helping you go from dreaming of a clearer mind, a cleaner home or office, a quieter life, etc. to living it. In this first chapter, we will do an in-depth assessment and discussion of the different *kinds* of clutter—namely physical, noise, digital, mental, and extraneous clutter.

All these types of clutter should be considered and evaluated continuously throughout your life. As the almighty "they," whoever *they* are, say, "Organization is a journey, not a destination." So, after learning about the different kinds of clutter, feel the freedom to sit with them, and little by little, implementations to improve will start piling up and lead to significant changes in your lifestyle. The evolution will never stop if you continue to allow and hold space for it!

Physical Clutter

This might go without saying, but physical clutter is exactly what it sounds like—excess items in your home, art studio, workspace, or anywhere else that you frequently occupy. It can be anything, such as pots and pans you never use, clothes you haven't worn in years, toys your children no longer play with, crusty paintbrushes, expired food...anything in your space that no longer serves its intended purpose.

However, physical clutter can also be considered those items that you have too much of. For instance, perhaps you have more jeans that you can practically wear and wash within a week. If that seems crazy to you and your lifestyle, maybe it's time to consider donating your less favorites to those in need who would get good use out of them. Another great example is shoes. This can go for all genders. An inspection of the footwear that you *actually* wear can be jarring when confronted with the dozens, if not more, pairs in your closet. Again, wouldn't it feel better to know someone was getting use out of them—instead of having them just collecting dust in your home?

Moreover, please be aware that the "rules" for deciding what physical items in your spaces are no longer necessary are unique to you and your lifestyle. Only you will truly know what things remain practical and serve a purpose for you.

But in that same breath, once that inner voice speaks to you and says whatever item you're currently focusing on is no longer needed, don't hesitate to toss, recycle, or donate it (depending on what it is and what state it is in).

Here are some tips for removing physical clutter:

- **Decide What You Want to Declutter**

When doing this, try to focus on specific locations instead of entire rooms. So, if you decide to start in the kitchen, don't simply focus on "kitchen" as a whole. Instead, it will seem easier to tackle when you narrow it down to smaller areas—like pantry, cupboards, fridge, etc.

(Pro tip: It can be helpful to photograph entire rooms to determine which areas need the most urgent attention. And it will serve as a satisfying before and after once the room is organized to your liking.)

- **Plan Your Day**

This is in a similar vein as the first point, but once you decide the areas in a room you want to tackle, plan your day (or weekend) in extreme detail, including setting times in which you should be done with each task. This will help you stay accountable and motivated. But don't forget to also pencil in little breaks for coffee, stress walks around the block, or anything else you might need to keep chugging along with your cleaning.

(Pro tip: Starting the day with something small that will give you a "quick win" can help you gain momentum.)

- **Sort Items into Three Piles**

Organizing will likely feel less stressful and more effective if you have a clear and designated spot to put things. For example, piling junk on top of the things you want to donate or keep won't help anyone. So, when you decide what to organize, establish three piles: keep, donate/sell, and discard.

- **Choose What to Pass On**

For most, this can be hard. Especially when an item that is taking up valuable space was gifted to you by a loved one or has other sentimental value to you. But the good news is 1) you don't have to tell people where certain gifts they've given you went and 2) you don't have to get rid of everything. In regard to the second point, you can create a little box labeled "Memories" to keep special items, like your garter from prom, tickets from when you saw your favorite band for the first time, love notes, pictures, etc., in.

(Pro tip: Aside from the things that may not have much function in your life but still have special meaning, anything else should be assessed on their level of necessity in your life. Say you have a whole shelf of candles that are taking the space of something else, like precious photo albums filled with pictures of your children throughout the years. In that case, the candles can probably go.)

- **Decide What to Keep**

Like with the memory box we just mentioned, organizing isn't just about tossing or getting rid of the things you no longer need. On the contrary, it's also aimed at showing you things you may have forgotten about that are useful, bring you happiness, and/or spark the joy of old memories. For example, throughout the cleaning of your closet, you find a goofy old sweater that you and your friends wore for a dance during a high school assembly. You might want to keep that, perhaps in tandem with a photograph, to show to your children someday to prove how silly you were in your youth. Again, that is why this process is so highly specific to you. To some, such an item might instantly be something to be thrown away or donated. But to others, it is really symbolic and something worth keeping.

- **Get Rid of Items Quickly**

Once you've decided what to get rid of, you should either throw them away, drop them off at a recycling or donation center, or put them online for sale as soon as possible. This is because holding onto them for prolonged periods of time doesn't help you get more organized. Instead, you'll just have bags of stuff around your house. Furthermore, the longer the items stay in your home, the more likely they are to accumulate back into your now-tidied drawers and closets.

Pro tip: If you are looking to donate clothes, please take extra care to make sure that the organization you're donating to is either non-profit (meaning the items will likely go to people in need) or for-profit (which will use the funds from selling them to benefit others, such as the National Cancer Center, which has donation boxes that state the proceeds go toward the researching for a cure.)

- **Utilize Storage Solutions**

There are plenty of attractive decorative boxes, stackable drawers, and other items that make storing things—especially seasonal decorations or clothing, extra sheets and towels for visitors, etc.—easier and more appealing to the eye.

- **Develop a System**

While organizing your things, putting labels on different bins or folders can help you relocate and remember what things are inside. For example, old tax documents or Christmas decorations that you need or want to keep can be placed into one designated place, labeled, and then found when needed.

- **Celebrate Your Wins**

As touched upon earlier, it's great to acknowledge and celebrate every success (no matter how small) when organizing your space. It might be a good idea to pause after every successful day and reflect on all of the good that you did for yourself.

Noise Clutter

This type of clutter can refer to two things:

- The overwhelming "noise" of criticism or responsibility in your life that can come internally or externally; or

- Actual noises that irritate you or keep you from enjoying your life.

"Noise"

This "noise" can be hard to wrap your mind around, but we'll do our best to help. Think of the things in your life that drive you crazy—like the fact that you can't seem to make it to work on time, you have a hard time saying no to plans you really don't want to participate in, or you don't hit your workout goals for the week. Anything you set as a goal but don't accomplish can result in detrimental internal dialogue and/or the external criticism of others.

Neither outcome is desirable. So, sticking to your goals and ambitions is a great way to alleviate this kind of "noise" clutter.

Further, having too many things going on at once can cause a kind of buzzing or other sound to appear in your head. That's the result of stress and being overwhelmed. If you find yourself in this position, talk to someone about how your load can be lightened at home or work. You can also make a list of things and cross them off one by one instead of looking at everything you have to get done in a vacuum.

Actual Noise

If you are like most people, you've lived in a duplex, dorm, or apartment sometime in your life. And if you have, you've also likely encountered a neighbor who plays music too loudly, hosts loud parties, has a heavy tread, or otherwise just produces a sound that irritates you. This is actual noise clutter.

If you feel comfortable addressing the issue personally, you should do so. But if not, that's what resident assistants and landlords are for.

You can encounter similar situations in other aspects of your life—at work, at the gym, etc. If it's a situation you can handle by speaking with the person responsible for producing the loud sounds, that's great. But if not—like if the music in a gym is too loud for your liking but the other patrons seem to have no issue with it—maybe it's time to find another place to work out or invest in some sound-canceling headphones if they are allowed in that establishment.

If you have sensitive hearing or get upset by loud noises, you may consider avoiding places like concerts, fairs, trampoline parks, or anywhere else where noise is inevitable. However, if you find that your sensitivities are ruining the overall quality of your life, you should consider speaking to your doctor or a therapist to address underlying issues and get help going forward.

Digital Clutter

Like the previous section, digital clutter can also come in two forms.

- Having too many screens in your life (constant attention on laptops, televisions, smartphones, etc.).

- Having disorganized filing on your laptop, desktop, phone, or tablet and having bloated email inboxes.

Too Many Screens

Whether at work or play, and whether it's our phones, computers, TVs, or tablets, it seems we're always looking at a flat surface that projects or reflects light.

Unfortunately, if your job requires you to look at a computer screen for long hours at a time, there isn't a whole lot you can do in terms of eliminating your screen time. However, you can get special glasses or activate your computer's settings to make the blue light less harmful to your eyes. Moreover, you can get special chairs or learn posture positions so that sitting for long periods of time does not put undue pressure on your neck, hips, and back.

If you have to endure extended screen times for your profession, you may want to consider trying to stay away from it at home. Reading a good book, drawing, playing with your pets, going for a walk, or cooking a new meal are great alternatives to reading the news, scrolling social media, or binge-watching a show.

The harms of too much screentime include:

- Damage to your eyesight.
- Interruptions in your sleep patterns.
- Increased risk for obesity.
- Poor posture (which can come with pain).
- Poor social skills.

- Headaches.

- Decreased attention.

- Declines in mental health.

- Poor core strength.

- Decline in brain development for children.

Disorganized Filing

Having endless unread emails, scattered desktop icons, and countless independent files are all examples of having a disorganized computer. Such clutter inhibits your efficiency at work because you'll have to spend more time than a well-organized person would to locate something.

Here are a few tips for getting your digital files and folders tidied up.

Establish a Clear Hierarchy for Your Folder Structure

This depends on the type of work you do. For example's sake, let's presume that you are a residential architect. In that case, your top-level folders may be "Bathroom Remodels," "Kitchen Makeovers," etc. Then, within those will be multiple folders and files pertaining to specific clients—"P. Johnson," "F. Smith," and "K. Williams."

Use a Consistent Naming Convention for Your Files

In a similar vein, create naming conventions that will make it easy for you to locate certain documents. Examples include:

- **Keywords:** Including specific words like "invoice," "contract," etc., in your files makes them easier to retrieve *and* it makes it clear to your client what you're sending to them via email.

- **Use Pascal Case:** If you're using compound words, capitalizing each first letter can make it easier to read. For example, "Johnson_AmendedAgreement" vs. "Johnson_Amendedagreement."

- **Add a Date:** Starting each file with the date (e.g., yyyy.mm.dd. or yy.mm.dd.) of the correspondence, signatures, or whatever will automatically list them in chronological order in your folder.

- **Include the Version Number:** This is as simple as adding "v1," "v2," "v3," etc., to multiple iterations of the same document to locate the most recent (and likely current) version.

- **Sequential Numbers:** If you want to arrange your files or folders in a particular order, adding a leading zero before each number (e.g., 01, 02, 03) will help you accomplish that.

- **Add "AA":** Another hack for organizing your files is by adding "AA" to the one you want at the very top. This will make finding your most important or most-used file easy to locate time and time again.

Add Tags

Suppose you are a cake decorator, and you take pictures of your most impressive work to post them on social media and other purposes. You can add tags in addition to folder and filing structures. For example, you could add tags like "Birthday Cakes," "Wedding Cakes," etc., to quickly pull up examples for a prospective client.

Delete or Archive Unnecessary Files

At the end of every week or month, designate some time to go through folders and delete, rehome, or otherwise archive files you no longer need.

Keep Your Email Under Control

- Set up filters to funnel certain emails to different folders.
- Unsubscribe to spam.
- Clear out your inbox.
- Consider setting up two addresses: one for the things you want to be subscribed to, and another that you only give your friends and your family.

Mental Clutter

Your mind becomes congested and unorganized when it is churning out too many thoughts—especially when they are unwanted, such as every "what if" excuse not to do something that will only improve your life (like exercise or eating healthy—and harsh self-criticism. Mental clutter can also occur when you are juggling too many tasks at once.

A great way to eliminate mental clutter is by journaling to get your thoughts outside of your body and onto paper, meditating, going for a walk, making to-do lists, reducing the number of decisions you have to make, limiting screen time, setting priorities, and any other coping method you find useful in finding peace during the day.

Extraneous Clutter

This refers to anything in your life that doesn't seem to have a place. These things can be in your vehicle, in your purse, under your bed, in your yard, or anywhere else.

Other Classifications

There are other ways in which people categorize clutter.

- **Homeless Clutter:** This is clutter in your home that doesn't have a designated spot. Later on, you're going to learn what we mean by "treating everything like a fork," and its purpose is to avoid this in your house.

What to Do: Find a designated space for each item that you own. But if you can't, perhaps it's time to consider getting rid of the overflow items.

- **Fantasy or Aspirational Clutter:** These are things like weights, yoga mats, roller skates, or anything else that the fantasy version (or ideal version) of yourself would have *and* use. However, if you don't actually use them, they have no business being in your home. Clothes that don't fit you anymore or no longer align with your lifestyle and unused art/hobby supplies fall into this category.

What to Do: Be honest and real with yourself. Say it's clothes that are too small for you. Are you really going (and are you physically able) to take the steps to lose the extra weight in order to fit into them? If yes, you have to start now. If no, it might be time to part with them. However, this is certainly not a self-hate exercise. Let the shirt or pair of pants go with love. Your body, which is the vessel in which you are allowed to be part of this world, once loved and looked good in them...but that isn't the case anymore. Maybe you had a baby, started taking a certain kind of medication, or suffered an injury and haven't been able to work out as often, etc. Whatever the case may be, if you're happy and healthy in your body, that's all that's important. Or maybe it's a pottery wheel that is taking up space in your garage. Ask yourself, "Am I really going to dedicate the time to learning how to use it?" If yes, start now. If no, find it another home where it will be cherished and used.

- **Guilty, Gifted, and Inherited Clutter:** Do you hold onto things like the nonsensical Mother's Day artwork that your children made you five years ago or that old clock that your father-in-law gave you but you've always hated? Those are examples of things we hold on simply because we feel like we have to. But the truth is that you don't. Of course, you'll probably want to have some childhood doodles and cards, and if that clock was dear to your partner's father or holds significance for him or her, you might consider holding onto it. But for anything that you're comfortable with pitching, you should.

What to Do: Nobody wants to disrespect family members by throwing out heirlooms and gifts we've received from them. One way to skirt around this is by asking around and seeing if someone else wants Grandma's doll collection or your mom's tea set that she bought when she was eighteen. If they say no, then discuss whether or not *anyone* in the family needs to keep the item(s). If yes, perhaps you can consider upcycling it into something you will use. For example, say your grandfather had a beloved pocket watch that he carried everywhere with him. You can easily turn (or have a professional do it) the face, hands, and other parts to create jewelry like earrings, necklaces, bracelets, etc. That way, you'll always have a piece of your grandpa with you, and you can look at the jewelry with fondness and in memory of him when you wear it.

- **Identity Clutter:** This is one of the hardest to recognize, and to do so, you have to have a lot of self-awareness work. This type of clutter refers to the things you hold onto simply because they feel like they're a part of you (or the person you used to be or want to be). However, it's different from fantasy clutter because it can be stuff that was useful and used at one time. A great example of this is stay-at-home mothers. Sometimes, even after their children have grown into teenagers or even adults, they have a hard time getting rid of little books, toys, or anything else their child holds dear. That's because they still identify as the mother of young children. But the harsh reality is they aren't anymore. As you'll read several times in this book, keeping *some* mementos are fine. But it's best to limit yourself to one small box of those. Anything else quickly starts to resemble clutter.

What to Do: It's simple (the solution...not always the process). Keep the small number of things that hold sentimental value, and either gift, sell, donate, or toss the rest.

- **Lazy Clutter:** If you're the kind of person who takes something out of a cabinet, drawer, closet, etc., and just leaves it out, you likely have lazy clutter around your house. That's not a judgment, it's just the truth. Lazy clutter is anything that has a home but is not currently in that designated spot. Taking the brief amount of time it takes to put things back after you're done using them will eliminate this issue and leave you with a less cluttered house.

What to Do: This one is also a bit of a no-brainer. Just try to be better about cleaning up after yourself.

- **Other People's Clutter:** This is probably one of the most infuriating types of clutter—your friend's, your family member's, or whoever else's junk that was dumped on you for whatever reason.

What to Do: Never, ever get rid of someone else's belongings without their permission. But this does not mean you can't give them warnings. For instance, suppose your friend left their Beanie Baby collection at your house (yes, this is a very specific example, but roll with it). You are a minimalist and don't want that kind of clutter in your house. Once your friend fails to come to pick them up a few times, you tell him or her that if it isn't gone in, say, a month (make it long enough to be reasonable on both your ends), you're going to take it into your own hands. That way, if they still don't get the crap out of your house, you are justified in getting rid of it.

***

No matter the type of clutter you have in your home, if it's bothering you and you want to observe a more minimalistic and cleaner house, find a way for you to feel guilt-free (or close to) and happy about getting rid of it. You'll thank yourself later.

Chapter Two

Make an Actual Plan

"By failing to prepare, you are preparing to fail."
~ Benjamin Franklin

To be successful in almost anything, you have to make a plan to execute and complete it. And organizing your life in all aspects is no exception! You are more likely to clear out your car, closet, cabinets, etc., if you pencil or type it into your calendar. Plus, the satisfaction of crossing it off or deleting it from a planner is oh, so satisfying!

However, when planning and organizing, please remember to stay positive. For instance, try to think of the outcome of clearing out your house instead of dreading the work it's going to take. This may seem hard at first, but with practice and consistency, you'll get the hang of it.

Frame Positively

We've heard an interesting concept regarding paying your bills: instead of seeing it as something you dread and money *leaving* your bank account, think of it as money you're being paid and investing in yourself. Or, if it helps, think of how it will positively affect your credit score. The very same mindset should be taken when planning to organize an area or your home, practice mindfulness, or any other method of decluttering yourself and your environment.

Rather than viewing the thirty minutes or few hours it will take to improve whatever can use some TLC as a chore or time you'd rather spend doing something more fun, picture how good you'll feel with a renewed mind or when you take that box of things that no longer serve you to a local shelter to help those in need. This will make undergoing the task so much more enjoyable and fulfilling!

If you need help making (and completing) plans, here are a few suggestions:

Get a Physical Planner

You can find one almost anywhere, and they come in all different price ranges, so you won't need to break the bank in order to get one. Physically writing tasks you hope to accomplish each day can help you stay accountable. (Plus, as we said at the top of this chapter, crossing off things on your to-do list once you've completed them is so wonderful!)

Keep a Large Family Calendar

For some, this may be a chalk or dry-erase board. Others may prefer a traditional paper calendar. Regardless, it should be placed in a focal point in a room that all members frequent (like by the front door, in the kitchen, etc.), and writing utensils should be easily accessible. This way, everyone in the household will, for lack of a better term, be "smacked" in the face by the plans and chores for the week/month.

Set Up A Digital Calendar

There are several products or apps you can purchase or download. We find it easy to use Google Calendar, which can sync with any other Google Workspace such as Gmail. You can add and share tasks you'd like to complete (such as decluttering activities) right there, and you can also set reminders to pop up in case you need them.

Psychological Benefits of Planning

Studies have shown that planning facilitates an increased rate of follow-through for two reasons.

- On a *mechanical level*, planning makes people anticipate and think of solutions to obstacles that may prevent them from performing their desired tasks.

For example, suppose you want to clear out your pantry to discard expired food and donate uneaten nonperishable food items (such as canned goods, syrup, peanut butter, honey, etc. You will likely have to carve out at least thirty minutes to a few hours, depending on how large your pantry is. However, you plan to do it on a Thursday night, which is also when your daughter has soccer practice. To fulfill your plan, you must coordinate with your partner or another family member to take her instead. Therefore, you're setting yourself up for success.

- On a *cognitive level*, making specific plans helps people remember their goals and pre-determine strategies for overcoming challenges they anticipate while pursuing their goals. These moment/behavior pairs take the following form: "If X happens, then Y will need to happen instead."

We'll use the same example of the mother who wants to go through her pantry on a Thursday night. Perhaps she anticipates that her partner, who has agreed to take their daughter to soccer practice, will end up working late that day. So, she plans to call her mother to ask that if her partner can't take the child, her mother will do it instead. This is a way for her to set up a contingency plan in case the initial plan becomes derailed.

Essentially, planning helps you stay committed to and plan ahead for potential obstructions that may keep you from achieving your goals. So, the next time you're feeling motivated to declutter a space, write or type that specific task in your calendar, designate the time you think it will take you, and clear the way for any obstructions ahead.

Psychological Damages from Poor Planning

Just as there are plenty of benefits for planning your and your family's weekly chores, failing to do so can also result in mental damage…and we're not just talking about the downward spiral a cluttered house can cause. We'll touch more on that later.

Letting Yourself Down

When you just think things like, "I really should clean out that closet" or "Ugh. The dishes in the sink are really piling up" but fail to make a concrete plan, you're more likely to just go about your day and forget about it. This is not upholding dignity—and yes, you should keep your word to yourself. It's just as important, if not more so, as keeping it to others.

When we keep our word, we build confidence in ourselves and our ability to navigate the world.

Diminished Motivation

For most people, taking a few seconds to write something down on a to-do list gives them that extra push to actually complete a task. When you don't, you can either forget it or push it to the side in favor of another activity.

How to Plan if You're Bad at It

Many of us find it hard to plan. Why? Well, sometimes our brains are just wired against it. Those who have natural brain dominance in the back-left part of their brain are said to be the most comfortable with making linear plans and sticking to them. That means people with brain dominance in another quadrant have to use one hundred times the energy to go into "planning" mode.

But does that mean that all hope is lost for them? Of course not!

Here are some things to consider when trying to improve your ability to plan:

Recognize Your Natural Strengths

If you find planning to be difficult or something you dread doing, chances are you do not have brain dominance in the back-left part of your brain. You can take the self-assessment in the book *Thriving in Mind: The Natural Key to Sustainable Neurofitness* by Dr. Katherine Benziger, or the more formal Benziger Thinking Styles Assessment, which can be found online. Then you may have a clearer understanding of why some things come so naturally to you while others do not.

Accept the Difficulty

Often, when we want something to be easy and it's not, we get frustrated and start thinking negatively about ourselves. But remember, you didn't choose which area of your brain holds dominance. And there's nothing you can do to change it. So, you might as well just accept it for what it is. This isn't the easiest thing in the world, but if you struggle with planning, having a little talk with yourself before engaging in the task—like saying, "(Your name), this is probably going to be hard for you. That's okay. It will take as much time as it takes. But you got this"—will establish a kind, forgiving, and realistic mindset with yourself. You just have to work through the feelings to get to your desired outcome.

Let Go of an All-Or-Nothing Mindset

People who find planning difficult often dismiss their ability to do so altogether and stop trying. Or they set unrealistic standards for themselves: if they plan something, they must follow it to the "t." Then, if they fail, they consider their efforts wasted. In reality, none of that is true. Life happens, so sticking to a plan isn't always possible. Instead, plans just need to be reworked and altered to fit your new reality/schedule. Moreover, it's a better use of time to take your successes and failures day by day.

Did you cross everything off your to-do list today? Awesome! Pat yourself on the back. But tomorrow is a new day.

Did you fail to wash the dishes because your class ran late? That's okay. Move past it. Tomorrow is a new day.

Find Systems That Work

Let's say you have a strong tendency for visuals (which is a common front-right brain dominance quality). You can use that to make planning easier and more effective for you. For example, you can write stuff on sticky notes, draw-erase boards, or mind maps. This will help you recognize and remember the tasks you want to complete. Or maybe you like spreadsheets (common in those with front-left brain dominance); you can use Excel or the Notes app on your phone to lay out, track, and check off your cleaning duties.

Please remember, there is no *right* way to plan. Experiment with a bunch of different methods, and then stick to the one that you find works best for you.

Borrow Other People's Brains

There's no shame in leaning on others who may find planning and organizing to be a breeze. And chances are, they enjoy doing those things, so asking them for a little help here and there is perfectly fine. They can either plan for you or give you tips on how they do it for you to adapt. Either way, this will probably save you time in the long run.

Please avoid asking overly critical people for this help. They may tear you down and discourage your learning process. Also, use caution and ask only for simple suggestions that will be easy for you to follow. You won't turn into an expert overnight—and a basic level of understanding is the best place to start.

Keep Trying

In order to be resilient, you need to be able to fall down but have the courage to get up time and time again. This requires self-compassion, refocusing when necessary, and processing and moving forward from frustration. Instead of telling yourself you'll never be good at planning, convince yourself that you will. But if it takes time, it takes time. The most important thing is that you're trying.

In this resilience rodeo, it's all about getting back on the horse, even if it sometimes feels like a bucking bronco in a (cluttered) corral. Laugh off the dust, and get back in the saddle. What else can you do?

Each attempt, no matter how modest, is progress. So, embrace the chaos and keep galloping toward your goal. With a bit of grit and a good sense of humor, there's no amount of peripheral chaos that can't be tamed.

Chapter Three

Stop Making Excuses

"99% of failures come from people who have the habit of making excuses."

~ George Washington Carver

Psychologists refer to making excuses as a self-handicapping behavior: it's something we do that hinders our performance and motivation. Once you understand that making excuses is normal and your brain's subconscious way of protecting you from anxiety and shame, you can acknowledge those little voices in your head that are keeping you from tackling that junk drawer or closet and then let them go.

Think about it. Excuses make us feel protected and less burdened...two things we as humans *love* to feel. And often when we make excuses, we blame external things. For instance, when explaining our inability to organize the house, we say we don't have enough time, need to go grocery shopping instead, it is too hard, etc. However, the comfort that excuses provide is a false sense of security. It's akin to putting a band-aid on a broken arm. While excuses might momentarily alleviate the sting of not tackling tasks, they don't solve the underlying issue: the clutter that continues to accumulate, both physically and mentally.

Excuses are often a mask for deeper issues such as fear of failure, perfectionism, or even attachment to possessions. We convince ourselves that it's easier to avoid the task than to face these underlying challenges. But in reality, the longer we put off dealing with the clutter, the more daunting it becomes.

It's important to recognize that excuses, while comforting, are procrastination in disguise. They keep us stuck in a cycle of inaction and dissatisfaction. To break free, start by challenging your excuses. Ask yourself, "Is it really true that I don't have time, or am I prioritizing other things over decluttering?" Often, you'll find that what seemed like an insurmountable barrier is actually a manageable obstacle.

Taking small, consistent actions can also help overcome the inertia excuses create. Instead of aiming to declutter your entire home in one go, start with one drawer or one shelf. These small victories can build momentum and prove to your brain that the excuses it's generating are not as solid as they seem.

Remember, the goal is progress, not perfection. Each step you take away from making excuses and toward decluttering your space is a step toward a more organized, serene, and functional environment. By recognizing and overcoming your excuses, you empower yourself to take control of your surroundings and, in turn, your life.

Good vs. Bad Excuses

Interestingly enough, psychologists deem excuses that are credible, maintain value for the goal, and generate sympathy for the excuse receiver to be good. They often result in sheltered self-esteem, lower levels of anxiety and depression, and a tougher immune system. Moreover, they may lead to a stronger performance (including a boost of self-control and focus) later on when similar scenarios arise again because the threat to your self-image is eliminated.

But bad excuses (also known as lies), which do not value the goal or sympathize with the receiver of the excuse, are detrimental. They may undermine your accountability and give the impression to others that you are conceited and do not value their time. And who wants to be around someone like that? Not many people.

So, if you notice that you are continually making plans and backing out of them for trivial and/or untrue reasons (i.e., "I'm sick," "My alarm clock didn't go off," "I forgot," etc.), it's time to address your self-accountability.

Not sure if you're making an advantageous or disadvantageous excuse? It's easy. Do you feel good about yourself after you make it? Chances are, if you're lying, you are going to feel at least a little lousy for deceiving someone.

Here's an example. You're a young parent, and your childless friends ask you to go to a concert at ten o'clock at night.

Here are some excuses that—if true—would be good ones to give:

- Not having anyone you feel comfortable with babysitting your infant

- Not being able to afford childcare

- Being too exhausted from the lack of sleep the night before

- Needing to get up early the next morning to take care of your child; staying out late would make you tired and less attentive to him or her

- Needing to stay home to care for your sick baby or partner

On the flip side, bad excuses would be any of the above that simply weren't true.

However, if you simply don't have the bandwidth at the time and don't want to go, that is also a good excuse. Unless this is going to put some kind of financial burden on them or keep them from doing something they were looking forward to doing,* it's perfectly fine to be honest with your friends. That's still a good excuse because you're being sincere. And if they are good friends, they'll likely understand and hit you up again the next time they plan to do something together.

* For instance, if it's just you and that other person going to a concert put on by their favorite band that they've been dying to see or a musical production they really love, which a majority of people wouldn't want to do alone, you should really try to find an alternative person to go in your place. If you can't, you should probably consider whether or not you'd feel good about yourself for backing out of the activity. As previously mentioned, that's the true test of a good vs. bad excuse.

Identifying Your Go-To Excuses

If you are just starting to maintain your dignity by only making good excuses, start noticing and potentially journaling your thoughts when someone asks you to do something.

Here are a few examples from a hypothetical healthy, able-bodied man named Richard in his fifties.

- Question from his daughter: "Do you want to go to the trampoline park with me and the grandkids?" Excuse from Richard: "I'm too old for that."

- Question from his elderly, widowed neighbor: "I'm having knee surgery next week. Can you please help me by making sure that my driveway and sidewalk are shoveled if it snows?" Excuse from Richard: "I'm too old to be doing that."

- Question from his wife: "I really want to go to Las Vegas. Can we plan a trip?" Excuse from Richard: "We're too old to be going to Vegas."

You're likely catching onto a pattern. Richard instantly goes to his age when coming up with an excuse not to do something. You'll notice that we noted up top that he is, in fact, perfectly well and capable of doing the things being asked of him. If he wasn't, or couldn't find an accommodation (like simply watching and enjoying his grandkids bounce on trampolines if he had bad knees and was afraid of hurting himself), then they'd be good excuses because they are self-preserving.

If your go-to excuses are not true, you should reconsider your mindset. Being old, for example, can be a state of mind (of course, given that you don't have ailments or valid concerns that keep you from doing certain things).

So, if you want to discover your favorite go-to excuses, undergo a similar exercise. Any time you say no to cleaning or organizing something in your life, document the reason. Not enough time? You have to do something else instead? Then, after you've discovered your own patterns, consider whether those are good (true) excuses (which they likely are not...at least not all the time) or bad (false) excuses.

Breaking the Habit

Unfortunately, while making excuses is a subconscious behavior—meaning that they are developed in a part of your mind that is outside of focal awareness—stopping the habit of making them is conscious, and you have to actively decide to stop.

However, the good news is that through tenacity and perseverance, even the hardest habit can be broken.

If you feel you could use a little extra help, below are six steps to changing a bad habit.

Identify Cues

Every habit has a trigger: something that cues it up. Think about it. Suppose you had what you considered a bad habit of eating too much chocolate. Well, that habit could be triggered by a stressful situation, such as a big project at work or a breakup. Chocolate might bring you the comfort you reach for during those times. For cleaning up and getting organized, the second you walk into your kitchen and see a pile of dishes, for example, you might feel overwhelmed and triggered to start making excuses in your mind as to why you shouldn't do them…you're too busy, you can always just do them tomorrow, you're a bad person (and a bad housekeeper) for not doing them, so there's no reason to even try, etc. Understanding your triggers is very important because they are what put your habits into motion.

Disrupt the Triggers

Once you understand your triggers, you can throw them off kilter. One of the greatest examples of this is about your alarm clock. If you find that you struggle with getting up on time because you're constantly hitting the snooze button, a way to disrupt that habit is by putting your phone across the room. That way, you'll have to physically get up (which will disrupt the snooze habit) and turn the alarm off.

To equate this to cleaning up after yourself, you can disrupt the habit of making excuses by tidying up a little bit more frequently. While it may seem like you're doing more cleaning, you're actually doing less. Plus, having a neat and organized house will motivate you to *keep* things that way. It takes less effort to clean a home that was already pretty clean in the first place, right? Right!

Replace

Replacing a bad old habit with a new positive one is a great way to eliminate the behaviors in your life that do not serve you. Say you've noticed that there's a weird smell in the back of your car, and you suspect that the aroma is coming from somewhere in the piling heaps of garbage you've discarded there. Each time you get in your car, you may feel triggered to think negatively about yourself. Well, a great habit to replace that with is just cleaning it up once and for all. Going forward, if a similar issue arises, you won't keep putting it off. Instead, you'll clean it immediately (or prevent it from ever getting to that state again). Being triggered to clean up a mess is much healthier than putting it off.

Keep It Simple

Breaking the habit of making excuses and putting off cleaning or organizing the spaces you occupy in life should be done in small and simple steps. We're not suggesting that you need to make it a habit to vacuum out every nook and cranny of your vehicle once a day. Instead, you should try to disrupt and replace your old habits of letting junk pile up on the floor. An example of a smaller step would be committing to get a little garbage can in the back that you will discard trash in and empty once a week. This will be much more successful than any large change you try to make.

Think Long-Term

Whenever you're struggling with abandoning a bad habit, it's best to think in big pictures. Like when you encounter the need to take out the trash. Why do you want to do that instead of keeping it inside your house? It may be because your long-term goal is to have a clean and tidy house to raise your family in. If that's the case, continually picture what your dream house will look like. Every day, you're making decisions and efforts, like taking the trash out when it's full, to get closer to that vision. Once you reach that goal, you'll have to continue working toward keeping your house that way.

Persist

What's great about our brains is that positive behaviors, when done over and over again, become habits. So, keep at them!

Here are a few examples of changing a negative habit into a positive one.

Habit	Identifying the Trigger	Disrupting the Bad Habit	Replacing the Habit and Persisting with a New, Simple One
After getting into bed, you take off your socks and throw them onto the floor, creating a graveyard of dirty socks by the end of the week. Your partner has expressed irritation about this, so you want to change it.	Getting into your bed before removing your socks.	Taking your socks off *before* getting into bed so you'll be more likely to throw them in the hamper.	Making the sock removal (again, before climbing into bed) part of your nightly ritual. Then, you can further add to this by doing something like putting lotion on the side of your bed and lathering your feet before hitting the hay. This will ensure your socks are off before getting into bed, and it will help your skin!

Starting out, or even after you're in the thick of changing a habit, it's perfectly fine to remember and repeat these steps as much as you need. Also, like so many things mentioned in this book, please remember that overcoming hard-wired habits is a unique process that depends on you and the behavior you wish to conquer. If it takes you a few tries to figure out what combination of identifying cues, disrupting, replacing, keeping it simple, thinking long-term, and persisting when it comes to making excuses, that's okay.

Always give yourself the grace of being a human. Oh, and don't be afraid to laugh a little along the way! Life is messy and hard at times. Finding the humor in the darkness and mundane is a powerful gift.

Chapter Four

Declutter Your House

> "The best way to find out what we really need is to get rid of the things that we don't."
>
> ~Marie Kondo

We went over tips and tricks for organizing personal clutter in the first chapter, but we're going to dive even deeper into this one.

When it comes to doing just about anything besides laying around and binging your favorite show, you need motivation. That's especially true for some when it comes to removing the clutter from your home.

And the unfortunate part is that once the problem is created, it can seem like letting it persist is the easier solution. But that's not true. As mentioned above, it takes a lot more time and effort to start from scratch in a filthy home.

Try to picture it. You live in a home with animals that shed quite a bit. What floor do you think will be easier to mop—one that is swept continually throughout the week, or one that hasn't been swept in some time?

Ding, ding! The correct answer is the first one. So going forward, if you find yourself struggling to stay motivated when it comes to doing simple things like sweeping your floor, dusting your bookshelves, etc., occasionally, just remember that. The more frequently you do it now will only benefit you, your home, and your happiness in the future.

Start Small and Work Outward

This is something else we've also touched on, but it bears repeating: when taking the leap to get your home more organized, it's best to start small, like arranging a set of drawers, pantry, etc., and then expand to other areas of that same room.

For example, let's assume you want to tackle the organization of your kitchen.

Step 1: Pick one area to start.

- Upper and lower cabinets
- Drawers
- Pantry
- Countertop areas
- Standalone shelves
- Island and/or kitchen cart storage
- Hanging storage
- Fridge
- Freezer

Step 2: Once you've made your selection, pull everything out and into a pile on your countertop, dining table, or any other clean place.

Step 3: Now that the space is empty, you can clean it. Whether it's a drawer, cabinet, or even the refrigerator,* you don't want to put things back into a dirty area. Start by dusting or using a vacuum attachment to get the dust and follow it up with an antibacterial solution.

Step 4: Depending on the space you've just cleaned, insert new shelf lining.

Step 5: Categorize the supplies you previously removed. Then, gather items you use more often and discard all broken or damaged tools.

Step 6: You've selected the items that you use more frequently; now consider where they should go in your kitchen. As you select these spots, think about how you use your kitchen. For instance, when placing spatulas, whisks, and other utensils that are often needed when cooking, think about having their home be a drawer you can easily reach while cooking.

Step 7: Before putting the supplies back in the cleaned drawers or cabinets, consider adding organization trays and dividers like the following:

- Utensil trays
- Roll-out drawers in low-level cabinets
- Stackable shelf inserts to tall cabinets
- Spice racks
- Pull-out trays for the fridge
- Vertical organizers for baking sheets, pots, and plates

The above are just some examples, and a simple Amazon search will bring up a whole bunch of ideas for you to consider based on your specific needs.

However, in general, investing in anything that will make it easier for you to see and access your kitchen supplies is a great way to get you to cook with them more (which, in turn, will save you the money you'd otherwise spend on takeout food).

Step 8: Cook! There's no better way to benefit from the fruits of the labor you just did than to prepare a delicious meal for you and your family.

Although we only went over reorganizing your kitchen area, the same steps can be used (just tweaked a little) for any room of your home. Simply pull everything out of your closet, vanity, nightstand, medicine cabinet, shoe rack, etc., inventory the things you use, plan to donate the things you don't, pitch those that are in bad shape or expired, clean the surfaces, install or replace lining if needed, assess the need for dividers or shelves, and go from there!

Honestly, once you start, you're probably going to find that it's hard to stop because organizing your belongings can be fun and overwhelmingly satisfying. Don't believe us? Try it!

*It's generally recommended to clean and sanitize your fridge every three to six months to ensure food safety and longevity.

A Comprehensive Guide

If you find that you need some extra encouragement while decluttering any room of your house, here are a few tips and tricks to consider trying.

- **Plan for Just Ten Minutes**

Especially as you're starting to go through your things, it can feel overwhelming. If that's the case, plan in ten-minute intervals. This will ensure that you'll get the task done because you'll have the stamina to do it. Ten minutes is all it takes to get the ball rolling. After that, if you want to do more, go for it. If not, that's okay too. Maybe tomorrow you can do twenty minutes or even thirty. Again, it isn't a bad excuse if you feel your body or mental health will decline with more work. Only you know what's best for you.

- **Have a Clear Goal**

Like the previous point, it can help to set a timer, but then also dictate what is to be done in that time. Are you going to go through everything in a kitchen drawer with the intention to pitch things you no longer need and reorganize everything you keep? Great! Whatever benefit and end result you want should be what you're striving for.

- **Take Action**

If your physical and mental health is in top shape and you feel like you *can* and *should* keep going with your decluttering (meaning that you're, for lack of a better term, just being a little lazy), one way to get that motivation is simply to do just that—keep going. Progress often leads to more progress!

- **Avoid Distraction**

Sometimes, when we want to avoid something hard like organizing our homes, everything else seems so much more appealing—be that doing your taxes, doing laundry, or whatever else. To avoid that, try to keep your focus on the clutter, your goal for cleaning it up, and the benefit you'll receive once it is all done.

- **Make It Fun**

Like we've said, decluttering doesn't need to be boring. Incorporating things like music, podcasts, or audiobooks can also help you stay focused and motivated. Further, once you make the habit of cleaning up your home fun, you're more likely to want to continue doing it in the future.

- **Plan Celebrations and Rewards**

Okay, we've suggested that you set ten-minute intervals to clean specific areas of your home. What we haven't said as clearly is how you should also schedule little celebrations after completing certain milestones. We talked about cooking a meal after decluttering your kitchen. Another example would be indulging in a self-care practice like taking a bubble bath with a nice face mask and glass of wine (if you're of age) after cleaning out your bathroom.

- **Get an Accountability Partner**

If you have a partner or roommate, it can be easier for both of you to stick to certain decluttering tasks if you agree on doing them together. If you live alone, call a family member or friend and commit to them that you will get whatever task done over the weekend. Feeling accountable to someone can be very motivating. It's easier for a lot of us to let ourselves down than others.

- **Consider What You Read, Watch, and Listen To**

Some people find motivation after watching *Tidying Up with Marie Kondo* or *Queer Eye* and watching other people transform their cluttered and dirty homes into neat, clean ones. Others may get inspired after watching *Hoarders* and want to declutter their homes in an effort to never get anywhere close to the place some of the people on that show get to (not that there needs to be any judgment of them—it just might not be the state of living you feel you'd rise and prosper in).

45 Easy Things to Declutter from Your Home

Below are several things—or categories of things—that may be easiest for you to look for, throw out, or donate when decluttering your house.

In General

- Trash

- Dead batteries

- Old light bulbs. (But be careful how you discard them…glass in garbage cans can be dangerous)

- Gifts you've received but never liked (remember, you don't owe the person who gave them to you explanations as to where they went).

- Free merch or "swag" you got from events—t-shirts with company names, water bottles, stickers, or anything else you were given in a draw-string backpack, perhaps, is useless if you aren't actively wearing or using them.

- Craft supplies you bought but never used. If you have yarn, drawing paper, or even an old sewing machine that is just gathering dust, it's probably best to give them to someone who will use them.

- Inflatable things like balls, pool toys, etc., that have irreparable holes in them.

- Pet supplies for a pet you no longer have (except for the few memorabilia items, of course, such as a collar you want to include in a frame with a photo of them, or if you're planning to get another pet of the same species down the road).

- Furniture that you cannot or do not want to repair.

In the Bathroom

- Dried-up nail polish. (There are products on the market that help to rehydrate them, but if you're not going to use it regardless—and be honest with yourself—it's likely best to just get rid of it.)

- Old or expired makeup

- Old toothbrushes

- Expired medications. (But be careful, especially with narcotics or other pain meds. If you're not sure what to do with a medication, take it to a pharmacy and ask. Better safe than sorry!)

- Towels that are in such bad shape that they cannot be used as rags.

In Your Bedroom

- Worn-out or unworn shoes

- Clothes that are beyond repair, are uncomfortable, or don't fit.

- Socks with holes in them or that don't have a mate.

- Purses you no longer use.

- Maternity clothes (if you're not planning to have more kids)

- Sheets that are pilling or have tears.

- Jewelry and other accessories you no longer wear.

- Books you've already read, have never read, or never plan to read again.

- Technology you no longer use. Old phones, tablets, Walkmans, etc. are just taking up space.

- Notes and books from classes you took in the past that won't be helpful in the future.

- Old calendars

- Used notebooks

- Old magazines

- CDs you don't listen to in your home or your car.

In the Living Room

- Framed décor that you bought but never hung up.

- Candles you don't like the scent of or that have "died" (meaning you can no longer light them).

- Decorative pillows that are past their prime (meaning they're dirty, uncomfortable to use, etc.).

- Old DVDs you don't watch anymore.

In the Kids' Rooms

- Games and puzzles with missing pieces

- Toys and books that they have outgrown (and you're done having children) or broken

- Coloring books that have been used up

- Broken crayons
- Dried-up markers
- Baby items (again, if you're finished growing your family)
- Old art projects (ask kids first if they're likely to be upset by this).
- Broken backpacks

In the Garage

- Tools you no longer or never have used.
- Dried up materials like paint, glue, etc.
- Empty boxes.
- Extra supplies from projects that have been completed.
- Old bikes, roller skates, etc., that your kids have outgrown, broken, or just don't use

We would go over the items *in the kitchen* that can be located and perhaps easily tossed, but we kind of went over that already. To reiterate in a nutshell, it's anything that you don't use, is broken, missing a component, or is expired.

Also, none of this is to imply that it's easy for everyone to give these kinds of items away. They are just suggestions and starting points for people who feel stuck or need help getting started to declutter.

Moreover, remember that once you decide to throw away, recycle, give away, or donate, do all of those activities as soon as possible to avoid reincorporating "junk" back into your home.

What is Minimalism?

Minimalism is a lifestyle that embraces intentional decluttering and simplicity when it comes to personal belongings.

As a minimalist, you will be more careful about the things you choose to bring into or keep in your home, and you value the bare necessities—like only furniture that you use, multi-faceted gadgets in the kitchen, a limited amount of clothes in your closet, etc.

To outsiders, it may seem like an extreme way to live...but it's quite the opposite. Once you get the hang of it, you'll see that your life is much simpler than it was before.

Common Challenges of Becoming a Minimalist

We can't lie: it isn't the easiest thing in the world to declutter your home and become more of a minimalist. Here are some of the hardships you'll likely face.

- **Letting Go:** It is very difficult for most people to detach themselves from belongings that often hold significance and sentimental value.

- **Social Pressure:** We live in a culture that promotes materialism. It can be challenging to live minimally in contrast to that.

- **Maintenance:** As we've said, decluttering needs to be a constant effort, and you need to be vigilant in the things you allow into your home to avoid clutter from accumulating.

- **Creativity:** Everyone's journey to minimalism looks different, so you will probably have to get creative when navigating the utility of minimal possessions.

- **Judgment:** Again, we live in a materialistic world, so people may make comments against your lifestyle. Try your best to ignore them and just live your best life.

Unique Challenges of Becoming a Minimalist

Of course, everyone's life looks different, so some issues pop up from time to time when it comes to having a decluttered home. Below are just examples and tips for overcoming some of the unique situations you may find yourself in (that not everyone does).

- **Living Large:** Some people struggle with overbuying décor, clothing, and anything else when they live in big homes. However, you don't need to live in a tiny space to be a minimalist! Even those of you with million-dollar mansions can live with only the essentials in life. Here's how.

Having Small Children

It can be a challenge to keep a decluttered home when you have children, but it is still possible. You just have to be even more disciplined. Below are a few things to consider.

It Starts with You: You cannot force your family members to join you in your minimalist lifestyle. However, you can lead by example by staying neat while not having expectations that your partner or children will follow it. As long as your life is as organized as possible, that needs to be enough.

- **Have Conversations:** Especially when your kids are young, you can talk with them about why you as a family own some things and don't own others. It shouldn't just be an implied way of living. But again, don't enter these talks with the expectation that they'll agree with you. Instead, be open to their feedback and opinions.

- **Enjoy the Simple Things:** Another way to lead by example is to do things with your kids that do not require a lot of money—like going for hikes, playing board games inside, or cooking a nice meal. This will teach them to enjoy the simple pleasures in life and not to always go to amusement parks, movies, etc.

- **View Setbacks as Opportunities to Grow:** Kids inevitably want toys, and they often go in phases about which ones they're into. For example, your child may suddenly want a ton of Barbie dolls. You might not give into these wants and desires, but other family members might. So, you may end up with tons of Barbies in your home. In that case, you probably won't win Parent of the Year for taking them away—which means you'll have to learn how to deal with the situation. Otherwise, you'll struggle. Remember, not everyone in your home has to agree with your minimalistic lifestyle.

- **Engage in Challenges as a Family:** You can pick one of the decluttering methods above or find another and undertake it together as a family. It may help motivate your kids to get rid of their old toys by telling them how other children—who are less fortunate than them—will get them instead.

- **Change Traditions:** If your family is like most, you engage in traditions, and one may be buying each other tons of gifts around the holidays. Of course, this might be a hard thing for people, especially kids, to get on board with ditching. But when you present the new tradition, like saving the money you would've used to buy gifts to go to Disney World or somewhere else fun,

The Benefits of Becoming a Minimalist

The great news is that, along with the many challenges,

- **Less Is (Definitely) More:** Keep spaces clear, and choose every piece in the room with intent.

- **Personalize It:** Being a minimalist is not necessarily about having stark white walls. Instead, if you want, you can play around with different colors and textures (through the use of fabric or other materials) to achieve a space that reflects your personality and sensibilities. Further, you can also customize your interior layout, furniture, and small amounts of decorative accessories.

- **Maximize Storage:** Sure, you'll have fewer belongings after the decluttering process, but that doesn't mean that you will eliminate clutter altogether. A minimalist's home often includes clever storage solutions that make rooms appear almost empty.

- **Embrace Clean Lines:** Clear tops, furniture with clean lines, and bare walls (for the most part) are highlights of a minimalist home because without clutter there's more room for the furniture and a limited amount of décor that you do have to breathe.

- **Invest in Quality over Quantity:** Because you'll have less, you can budget for nicer pieces.

Create a Neutral Base: The flow of a minimalist's house starts with a neutral base that creates a calm living space. For example, a neutral using white can also incorporate grays, tans, yellows, and beiges without feeling overwhelming.

Chapter Five

Declutter at Work

> "When you are overwhelmed, tired, and stressed, the solution is almost always less. Get rid of something. Lots of somethings."
>
> ~ Courtney Carver

Just as in your personal space, decluttering in the workplace should be a high priority and a regularly pursued goal. The sense of achievement and motivation garnered from tidying up your home can be a powerful catalyst when applied to your office and professional life.

In the realm of work, clutter not only disrupts physical space but can also impede mental clarity and productivity. A cluttered desk or an overflowing email inbox can be overwhelming and can significantly hamper your ability to focus and perform effectively. By adopting a systematic approach to decluttering at work, you lay the groundwork for a more organized, efficient, and less stressful working environment.

Start by evaluating your workspace. Does your desk serve as a dumping ground for papers, stationery, and miscellaneous items, or is it a well-organized area that promotes productivity? Organizing your physical workspace is the first step toward a clearer mind and a more structured workday. Implementing simple strategies such as regular filing, digitizing documents, and designating specific spots for various items can make a world of difference.

The same principles apply to digital clutter. An unmanaged digital space—be it your email, or online work tools—can be just as chaotic as physical clutter. Oftentimes *more* so! Regularly cleaning out your inbox, organizing files into clearly labeled folders, and unsubscribing from unnecessary email lists can streamline your workflow, making it easier to locate what you need and focus on the task at hand.

Remember, decluttering at work is *not* a one-off task but a continuous process. It involves regularly reassessing and adjusting your systems to ensure that they remain effective and relevant to your changing work requirements. By maintaining a decluttered workspace, you not only enhance your productivity and efficiency but also create a more pleasant and conducive work environment for yourself and your colleagues.

Psychological Benefits of Having a Decluttered Workspace

We've already mentioned a few helpful tips on how to stay digitally organized, and a lot of the tricks on organizing your home apply to your office as well. But what we're about to go into now are the actual benefits you'll experience as a result of having a decluttered office, including some that will help you become more productive, seem more presentable to coworkers and clients, have an overall decrease in stress, and more!

Time Management and Productivity

When your office is well organized, you tend to know where every digital and physical file is located, and you'll save a considerable amount of effort by not having to search for them for minutes or even hours on end. With all that extra time, you can catch up on emails, review that sales pitch you have to present, or just go fill up your coffee mug! Another thing to consider is clearing as many files, emails, etc., on your desk as possible. Because when it's cluttered, multiple things are vying for your attention at once.

Presentation

If you are like most professionals, you probably have coworkers and clients/customers who come into your office on the regular for meetings. Well, if that office is a mess with papers haphazardly piled up in random stacks or your inbox is overflowing, you will probably send a message to them that you don't have your sh** together. And most people prefer to work with those that they deem focused and in control of their lives. So, if you want to make a good impression, a decluttered office is one way to do it right off the bat. This may also boost your confidence when meeting with colleagues or clients.

Decreased Stress and Frustration

Having an organized office saves you from a lot of unnecessary stress. This is especially true for those who work in fields like law, medicine, finance, etc., that inherently come with high stakes. You don't need anything like a messy desk or misplaced file added to your shoulders. A little tidying here and there will help ensure that it won't, or will at least be far less likely to, happen.

More Space

This one is more straightforward—simply put, when you have a tidier office, you'll likely also have more space in that area as well. So, you will have room to take on additional client folders, things that make you happy, like pictures of your family, or just have extra space for nothing, which is certainly more calming than a mess.

Improved Immunity

Especially if it's been a long time since your desk and surrounding surfaces have gotten a good clean, doing so may remove harmful germs and bacteria, thus helping you stay healthy.

Developing Creativity

Studies have shown that having a cluttered workspace can have a dampening effect on pumping out innovative and inspiring ideas.

Decrease the Chance of Injury

Did you know that thousands of people are hospitalized each year after suffering from falls? Do yourself and your colleagues a favor by keeping your office and the surrounding areas as well organized as possible—and that means keeping boxes and other hazards off the floor.

If you aren't convinced yet, there really aren't any disadvantages to keeping an uncluttered office. On the contrary, keeping a clean and tidied one will make you better at your job, more desirable to clients, healthier, more mentally clear, and more confident in yourself and your ability to perform your duties.

Now, we can't tell you what to do...but if we were you, we'd take a good hard look at our office and see any areas that could be improved upon.

Tips for Decluttering Your Office

You can utilize several of the tricks and steps we've already discussed in regard to cleaning your home. But here's a specific list for you to refer back to, if need be:

- **Start Small:** Just like we've said when starting to organize your home, when you begin decluttering your office, you should pick one area—like a filing cabinet, desk drawer, a bookshelf, etc., and then work from there. Choosing larger areas may make you feel overwhelmed or cause you to lose your sense of accomplishment; finishing several small projects has the opposite effect.

- **Set a "Due" Date:** Think realistically about how long it's going to take you to clean up your office and choose a date (preferably a little later than you anticipate finishing...decluttering takes time, and sometimes more than you think) to have it all done, and do your very best to stick to that. For example, a great day to pick would be the day before a big client meeting. That way, you have motivation and a *point* for all of the work you're going to put in.

- **Be Kind to Yourself:** As we mentioned in the last point, throughout this entire process, you should think and speak kindly about yourself. Also, don't judge your workspace against anyone else's. What works for you and the work you do is unique to you. Moreover, think about incorporating decorations—such as a fake bouquet of your favorite flowers, pictures of your family and your pets, a poster with your favorite motivational phrase on it, etc.—into your space. A simple thing like that will make you feel more comfortable and more at home.

- **Labels, Labels, Labels:** Once you collect certain documents into a file or collect multiple files into boxes, make sure to either write or print descriptive labels and put them where they will be the most visible. For instance, say you work as a general practice lawyer and have a bunch of old, closed client files hanging around your office. You could collect them and bundle them together based on the type of case (divorce proceedings, estate and probate, personal injury, etc.) and put them into corresponding boxes with the area of law they dealt with, last names and first initial of the clients, case numbers, and the date range work was done. So, the label could read something like this:

>   PROBATE (CLOSED CASES)
>   Ehrens, H. CV03455
>   Coleman, A. CV0999
>   Johnson, P. CV00093
>   Williams, F. CV01118
>   02/03/19 – 12/15/21

That way, anyone, including you, can look at it and know exactly what's inside in case you need any of the documents for future reference. Again, different methods work for different types of work and different kinds of people. Make sure you find what works best for you and your office.

- **Be Resourceful:** There are plenty of types of storage containers. Performing a simple Amazon search or a trip to Target or Walmart may be enlightening to you as you work to organize your office. Also, you can ask office managers if there are any unused filing cabinets or other storage implements gathering dust somewhere that you could make use of. You never know!

Chapter Six

Declutter Your Mind and Habits

> "Clutter is not just the stuff on your floor – it's anything that stands between you and the life you want to be living."
> ~ Peter Walsh

As you've already learned, actions or thoughts that do not benefit you yet occur constantly do so because you've unintentionally made a habit of doing or thinking them. This may seem counterintuitive, but unfortunately, that's just how our brains work. We (unconsciously) decide that things like cleaning and decluttering our personal spaces are too hard and time-consuming, so we don't do them—at least not nearly as often as we should.

Why? Because habits are imprinted in our minds, and when we act on them (by walking past the dirty pile of dishes in the sink, for example), dopamine gets released and we feel happy. Having a dirty home may not make us feel pleasure, but the physical act of not cleaning and instead moving onto something we like doing does.

We hope this makes sense, but if not, never fear. We'll cover more and expand upon the concept in this chapter.

How to Develop Good Habits

The first step to getting rid of a bad habit and turning it into a good one is realizing that it exists in the first place. Remember a few chapters back when we talked about making excuses? We mentioned how making untruthful excuses is a bad habit that has to be recognized before it can be changed.

You'll likely also recall that we mentioned how the negative habit can be turned positive when flipped. So, instead of lying and saying you can't go out with your friends one night because you have to work late (again, this is only bad if it isn't true), you can be honest and say you're too tired.* This preserves your dignity and the friendship. On the same side of that coin, you don't want to make it a habit to continually say "yes" to plans and then back out of them at the last minute. That's disrespectful of other people's time and makes you look like a flake. You're likely to stop getting invited to places altogether.

We know, we know. This may seem easier said than done…and that's true to some degree. Changing a bad habit into a good one, or just developing a new positive habit, takes will, practice, and repetition. It's certainly not for the faint of heart.

* Make sure that saying you're too tired doesn't become a crutch or an excuse. You can use it once in a while, but if you care to preserve the friendship you have with that person, sometimes you have to suck it up and go out for dinner, to a concert, or whatever else they ask you to do with them. Of course, this shouldn't compromise your morals or anything. If a group of friends want to go out to a strip club but that's just not something you're into, that's fine; good friends should understand and respect your boundaries. But plans that have no consequence on your

values are different. Besides, in general, you should want to do things and be around your friends...that's why they're your friends, right?

Your Thoughts Are Your Reality

Your brain and what it thinks is so incredibly powerful. But this idea is so simple that most people miss it or fail to fully grasp it. We find that people who suffer from anxiety may understand this phenomenon better than those who do not. Here's an example: you once passed out momentarily, and now you are hyper-fixated on not having that happen ever again. Well, by constantly thinking "What if I pass out right now?" you are telling your brain that that's exactly what is happening (and what you *want* to be happening), and you'll likely find that you feel woozy. See? By worrying about something, you're telling yourself that's what the reality of the situation is...and your mind doesn't know the difference between fact and fiction.

So, thinking positively about yourself and your life will only make that become your reality. Pretty awesome, right? This doesn't only work for health, either. You can implement this habit into every area of life. That means that today, you can start telling yourself something you want to be—like, "I'm very wealthy." If you make that thought a habit, instead of wallowing in the debt or nominal amount of money in your bank account, you'll start to see money piling up around you. But be careful. It's not, "I *want* to be wealthy." No. "I *am* wealthy." Telling your brain and, in turn, the universe that you "want" something is meaningless. Tell it you already are what you want.

By retraining your brain to think that your life is the way you want it to be, you're tapping into your subconscious and telling it what you want—and it will deliver that! The same works for negative thinking...so please try to remember that.

The Power of Gratitude

Let's expand on the desire to become wealthy. Chances are, if you're like most, you have so much more in your life that supports you than you realize.

Want an example? Well, let us ask you this: do you have easy access to clean water? If the answer is yes, you are better off than a ton of people on this earth. That in and of itself makes you wealthy. You have something at your fingertips that others walk miles and miles for every day. What about a sturdy roof over your head? Do you have one of those? Again, if yes, goodness, you are so fortunate!

It doesn't have to be physical things. Think about your relationships. Is your mother still alive and healthy? Not everyone can say that. What about your romantic partner? Do you have one who treats you well? If so, you're blessed. Please act like it.

Thinking about things you may otherwise take for granted is a way to pay respect to the universe for everything it's already given you. And guess what? It will only continue to give you more once you acknowledge the gifts you've received.

The next time you're filling your water bottle at home, at work, or at the gym, make a conscious effort to remember how privileged you are to have that, and think, "Thank you, water."

The Power of Meditation

Many find that they are able to express gratitude and manifest the things they want through the practice of meditation. But meditation isn't just one thing—not even in the slightest, friends! We've been harping on and on in this book about how you are a unique individual, and that also goes for how you meditate effectively.

Some people find it easy to just walk or run through nature, take in the views, and think about everything the universe has given them and what they want to create in this world. Others act on what most people think when they hear the word "meditation," and they either listen to recorded audio and music prepared for by professionals or sit quietly in a room with their eyes closed* and concentrate on gratitude and the reality they are hoping to exist in.

Others still benefit from hypnotherapy. You've probably seen a hypnotist perform a show in person or online. They make people do crazy things like see someone as a *Sesame Street* character, hear positive things someone says about them as negative, etc. That isn't exactly what we're talking about. But it's similar in that you are altering what reality is in your mind. Again, this can be done alone and in silence or by a guided video/audio developed by a professional hypnotherapist.

No matter which way you choose to meditate, remember the goal is always to retrain the subconscious part of your brain to think and operate in a certain way.

Here's the magical formula:

Positive thoughts = positive outcomes. Positive outcomes = productivity.

(It really is that easy. But it also has to be unwavering, which is the challenging part.)

* If you want to learn how to get yourself into a state of hypnosis, there are plenty of videos online…but make sure you're learning from a licensed hypnotherapist.

Vibration

We're sure you've heard the saying, "You get what you give." Well, as we've already said, that's true when it comes to your thoughts...and it's also true when it comes to your vibrations, meaning the feelings you put out into the world (which come from your thoughts).

Let's say, for example, that you're feeling like a victim in life. Maybe you lost your job, you are behind on bills, and you swear that the world is against you. If you continue to mope and stew in that kind of thinking, that's exactly what you're going to get handed back to you. Although it may seem hard, feeling the *exact* opposite way is how you're going to get out of that rut: feeling like you are powerful and worthy of money and a good job.

Manifesting a Decluttered Life (Bringing It All Together)

So, now that you've read about gratitude, meditation, and vibration, you may be left asking, "What in the world does this have to do with me having a clean house, office, etc.?" Well, take a moment to think about that.

If you didn't know already, you now know the freaking awesome power you have inside of your skull. If you're constantly telling yourself that you don't like to clean or that you're just a messy person, that will be what, how, and who you are. Instead, try thinking positively about cleaning. See, smell, and taste the feeling of having a tidy home. Next, tell yourself that you are an organized and clean person. Guess what you're likely going to find yourself doing? Cleaning!

Imagine all the good things your ability to, enthusiasm for, and hard work while cleaning could bring to your life and the lives of others. That power is just waiting to be unleashed in the world...if you'll let it and start working toward a more positive way of thinking.

Say it with us. "I love to clean. I am a clean and tidy person. Cleaning makes me feel good." Congratulations! You're well on your way to having a decluttered home *and* mind.

However, please remember that this is a continual process that will take your entire life to master. So, take it day by day, hour by hour, minute by minute, and focus on doing the best you can.

Simple Ways to Practice Meditation While Cleaning

Many of us are very busy with work, wrangling our kids, etc., so setting aside time to be mindful isn't always possible. So, while you clean, try to think (and be mindful) of the following.

- **Practice Gratitude:** As you go through the motions of decluttering and cleaning your space, think about how fortunate you have been in your life to acquire your belongings, how grateful you are that your body is physically able to clean, and how you are ready to part with some things with peace and love. Maybe they've never served you or they are no longer able to serve you. Either way, think positively about how they will be recycled and turned into something another person will enjoy as you donate or sell them to someone who will treasure them. It's a little harder to think fondly of the future of an item that will end up in a landfill...but still, emotionally detach from it and send it on its merry way.

- **When You Clean, Just Clean:** Don't think about other tasks you have to do or anything like that.

- **Check in with Your Body:** Our bodies continue to function without our participation—our organs keep working, our lungs continue to help us breathe, our throats continue to swallow our saliva (yuck!), our hearts continue to beat, and our eyes continue to blink all without our conscious decision to do so. Plus, our bodies are constantly sending messages to our brains in the form of aches and pains. So, as you clean or organize a space, pause a moment and see what you notice. Are you stiff or sore anywhere? Do any of your joints hurt? This may alter the way you use part of your body—for example, say you realize that your knees are hurting. In that instance, you may not want to be on them for long periods of time as you clean a floor or go through some clothing. You may choose to use a mop instead and set everything up on your bed for you to sit and dig through.

This can also be useful when deciding what to keep or get rid of. Listen to your body. If something makes you feel gross versus warm and happy inside, that's telling you something about it.

- **Pay Attention to Your Emotions:** Roxette said it best: "Listen to your heart!" Just like our bodies, our emotions tend to operate without much conscious effort from us. As you clean or declutter your home, make sure you're paying attention to how you're feeling. Are you gleeful or filled with sorrow as you address certain areas of your house or decipher whether or not to hang on to an old sweater? Try to take control back and "force" yourself to feel happy while doing these activities. They are for the benefit of your physical and mental health, after all!

Moreover, try to capture the feelings you have after you're done decluttering. You'll want to remember that for the future because it can motivate you.

- **Fire up Your Five Senses:** One of the easiest ways to feel present is by carefully observing everything that's going on around you. As you declutter, notice what you smell, hear, feel, etc. Take notice of the senses you enjoy because replicating them can help motivate you to clean in the future. For instance, perhaps you really like the smell of a certain cleaning solution. You will probably be more inclined to use it if you enjoy that your house smells of it. Things like that can make a real difference in your life.

- **Practice a Centering Exercise:** If you find your mind wandering as you work to declutter or clean your home, you can come back to the here and now by taking a thirty-second break to do the following. This exercise will help you feel more present and focused.

    - Close your eyes.

    - Put both feet on the ground.

    - Sit up straight and imagine that a string is pulling you straight up through the top of your head.

    - Do a body scan to see if you're holding energy anywhere, and if you are, release it.

    - Take a deep breath in and out.

    - Repeat the breath, but this time, imagine that all of the tension in your body is being flushed down—into the ground.

- **Focus on Your Breath:** Yet another way to center or calm a cluttered mind is by taking a minute to observe your breathing. Remember, your body does this without you having to think about it, but it nevertheless corresponds to thoughts and feelings that we're having. Ask yourself if your breathing is shallow or deep. Either way, take five deep breaths and pay close attention to your inhales and exhales. Repeat this process several times throughout the day as you feel necessary.

Paying close attention to the feelings and thoughts that we have while tidying our houses is integral if you want to change the task into something you do often and even look forward to doing.

Chapter Seven

Keep Your Sh** Decluttered

> "The more I examine the issue of clutter, the more effort I put into combatting it because it really does act as a weight."
>
> ~ Gretchen Rubin

So, you've gone through the trouble of combing through your belongings and cleaning your house or office. Marvelous! Celebrate that. But after that celebration, sit down and implement changes and schedules aimed at keeping things clean and organized.

Time Management

We have brought this point up a few times in the book already, but planning ahead and managing your time effectively are key to keeping you focused, productive, and motivated.

At the start of every week or day, sit down with your calendar, physical or digital, and add "chores" for yourself on certain days, allotting the time you anticipate each activity taking. For instance, suppose you get off work early on Wednesdays. On that day, in general, you can plan to do your laundry, fold your clothes, and put them away. Take into consideration how long it usually takes you to do all of that, and then note it— *Wednesday, June 12— Work 9 to 2; Laundry 4 – 6:30.* Next, consider what, if anything, is feasible to achieve the next day. After you do this a few times, you'll probably get a solid schedule established that you can follow week after week. Of course, things happen, and life is unexpected. But for the most part, you should be able to stick to this plan.

That will all encourage you to complete the task and help you from being overloaded by the burden of having to clean your entire home or office in a day or two, which might make you revert to old habits of negative self-talk and avoidance of messes. That's not what we want!

Start Small

It might feel like we're beating a dead horse at this point, but please remember to start small. However, that is not to say that you should avoid the bigger projects forever. The run-down bathroom you've neglected in the past will need to be remodeled, the living room with chipping paint will need to be repainted, and going through the seemingly never-ending storage containers in your basement will need to be tackled. Think of your house as a leaking pipe. Applying small patches on it will work for a while. But at the end of the day, all you'll have is a patched-up pipe that is likely still leaking.

The same goes for your home or office. Little tasks and clean-ups will work for a while, but for the job to be done, it *all* needs to be completed and maintained. Moreover, the façade of a clean house is only that—a false appearance. If you have one area of the house—especially one that is out in the open for visitors to see—all neat and clean, but behind another door there are piles and piles of junk, you do *not* have a clean house. Instead, you have a clean room and the *appearance* of a clean house. They aren't the same thing.

Check-Ins

We've already suggested that you practice mindfulness and make deals with your roommates, partners, family members, friends, or anyone else you feel will hold you to things when beginning your decluttering journey. But it's just as important, if not more so, for you to hold yourself accountable to…well, you.

Recall what we said about making bad excuses to other people, an activity that will make you seem untrustworthy and deceitful. You do the same thing to yourself when you make a goal or plan and fail to obtain or act on it.

So, if you decide to clean or organize a certain area of your home on a particular day and time, you should try your absolute best to do it. Don't let yourself down. You are all you've got at the end of the day; you might as well be dependable.

Here are some steps you can take when checking in with yourself.

- **Close Your Eyes:** For some of us, this is one of the easiest ways of going inside our own bodies and minds. Closing out the entire world helps us focus on what we're feeling, thinking, etc.

- **Take a Few Deep Breaths:** Breathing in slowly through the mouth and then out through the nose is a method of going even deeper into our thoughts and removing distractions from the outside world.

- **Zero in on You and Your Body:** Is your heart racing? Are your palms sweaty? These kinds of things are trying to communicate something to you, and you'd be wisest to listen and figure out where this *dis*-ease is coming from.

- **Ask Check-In Questions:** Take a moment and ask questions like:

    - Do I feel good about the current appearance of my house?

    - Do I feel anxious, stressed, or worried about the amount of clutter in my house?

    - If a friend of family member were to walk into my house right now, how would I feel? Happy? Nervous?

    - Do I feel like I'm growing in my decluttering journey?

    - What do I need to forgive myself for this week?

    - What did I do this week that was a step in the right direction when it comes to the goal I want to achieve?

    - How can I be tougher on myself and my cleaning habits?

    - How can I be kinder to myself and my cleaning habits?

In answering, trust your gut, and don't dwell on each question for too long. How you instantly feel is how you feel. If it's positive, great job. However, if it's negative, that's also awesome! You are showing yourself areas in which you can improve for the benefit of a cleaner, healthier, and better life. Further, you may want to take some additional time to journal about the feelings and thoughts you had during this process. It may help you to understand where you're at, and it will also serve as a way for you to measure your progress.

Just like penciling in the dates and times for organizing or cleaning, you can also add times and alarms for you to do these check-ins. It's funny. We think and think all day, but we so often forget to talk and listen to ourselves. We're hoping you're learning through this book just how important self-awareness and self-talk are in every area of your life.

14 Simple Habits for Staying Decluttered

We've laid out a few tips for staying decluttered, but here are some additional ones.

Never Leave a Room Empty-Handed

When going from one room to the next in your house, take a second to scan where you are. Do you see anything that you could take and return to its designated spot in the next room?

Suppose you're going to go from the living room to the kitchen. Look around and see if there are any dishes, mugs, utensils, etc., that you can bring with you. Or when you're putting your child to bed, grab any toys, books, or blankets with you to their room. Making your trip perform double duties like this is a great way to stay organized.

Participate in the "One-Basket Tactic"

Find or purchase a bin, basket, or container big enough to hold a stack of papers. Then, put it in a central location of your home. Throughout the week, you can place items such as mail, school permission slips, bills, library books that need to be returned, or anything else—that is not urgent but will require more time to address than you currently have.

Then pick a date every week—some people find Sunday evenings best, but whatever works best for you is totally fine—and plan your week in accordance with the papers you've collected. For instance, say you have three bills due next week. Schedule the payment of them. At the same time, think about the goals and other tasks you want to complete every week.

Practice "One In and One Out"

When you buy something new, think about it as something that needs to take the place of something that's already inside your home (as if you only have room for a limited number of things and that limited number only). For it to "fit," you'll need to get rid of something else. This is an excellent way to stay decluttered and bogged down with excessive stuff.

Do a Ten-Minute Clean Each Day

Did you ever watch *Big Comfy Couch* as a kid? If you did, you probably remember Lunette the Clown doing ten-second cleanups. However, she had the magical ability to fast-forward time, something we mere mortals cannot do. A ten-minute cleaning is more effective for us.

Set a ten-minute timer every day and clean one area of your house—be it the kitchen table, your dresser, your child's play area, whatever. By tidying a little every day, you're less likely to become overwhelmed with clutter.

Take Twenty-Four Hours to Consider Purchases

Mindful shopping can be hard; there's no denying that. But you'll find that taking just one day to consider buying that new pair of shoes, scarf, sweater, etc., will not only help you manage your money but will help you keep your living space clutter-free.

In those twenty-four hours, consider whether you really need something else brought into your home, ask yourself if you really have the space for it, and, if you're participating in the "one in, one out" technique, consider which item you'll remove in order to "make room" for the new item.

If It Takes Two Minutes, Do It Now

Many of us constantly put things off that don't take much time to accomplish in the first place—like failing to take a suit jacket off and hang it back up in your closet instead of flinging it across a kitchen chair. By doing little things like this, we are creating more work for ourselves in the future. So, anything that will take you two minutes or less to do, just suck it up and do it now. You'll find that your space is much cleaner, which will put you at ease and keep your stress at bay.

Make the Bed

It's great for your mindset to start the day by completing a task…even one as simple as making your bed. You'll live the rest of your waking hours in "clean" mode, and doing small things like that around your home or office will seem like nothing (and maybe even enjoyable) to you.

Put It Away When You're Done With It

Throughout the day, as you accomplish things such as doing your makeup, making lunch, grooming the dog, etc., put the instruments you used back where they belong. Your blush, eyeliner, lipstick, and powder should go right back into the medicine cabinet or vanity where you keep them. Bowls, utensils, and pans should be cleaned and returned to their cabinet or drawer as soon as you're done cooking and eating.

By making it a habit to clean up after yourself right away, you will avoid accumulating clutter, dirt, and grime in your home. Plus, it will save you so much time in the future!

Halfway Is Better Than Not at All

This one relates to the last point. Unfortunately, sometimes you're simply in a hurry. You could be running late for work, your child's soccer game, or a doctor's appointment, and you don't have the time to put all your makeup back where it belongs. Well, in that case, doing *some* (as much as you possibly can in the time frame you have) of the cleaning up is better than none at all. Remember, it's all less work you'll have to do upon returning home.

Finish One Task Before Moving on to the Next

Especially with the fast timing of life, we tend to have the attention span of a goldfish, and cleaning around our house is no exception. So often we are in the middle of something and stop when we see a separate pile of dirt or mess. Giving into those impulses will only add to the time it will take you to tidy up…if you ever come back to the project you ditched in the first place.

Borrow Instead of Buy

We fall into patterns of clutter when we purchase things and hold onto them forever when we could've just borrowed and returned them to someone. A great example of this is books. Look at your shelves right now. Chances are they are filled with books you've never read or read and plan to never read again. Of course, it's fine to hold onto a few of your favorites, but other than that, you're likely better off borrowing from your local library, a friend, or a family member.

However, when you do borrow things, whether it's a book or anything else, keep a record of what you borrowed, who you borrowed it from, and when. Resentments over unreturned items, even without your malicious intent, are very real. And if you don't value someone's possessions, it in turn can make them feel like you don't value them.

Say No to Free Stuff

Like resisting a good impulse buy, saying no to free things can also be really hard. But the problem is, if you accept something free and don't really need it, it is likely to just become clutter. Oh, and you're also running the risk of taking something from someone who could use it. Saying *no* to the free tote bag, water bottle, or whatever—again, unless you could make good use of it—is likely in your best interest.

This also goes for accepting hand-me-downs from family members and friends. Yes, this can be even more challenging than saying no to a stranger. However, you can't let guilt allow junk into our homes and lives. You also need to respect other people's space. So many grown adults have countless totes full of childhood toys and trinkets sitting in their parents' basements. If they took the time to go through it all, they'd probably toss most of it out. But by failing to look through it and get them out of their parents' way, they are being disrespectful and selfish. If this describes you, please take this as your sign to help the poor woman and man who raised you and get your junk out of their house!

Accept That You're Never Going to Fix It

Do you have a collection of items you've had set aside because you intend to fix them? Like that elephant statue your sister brought back from China for you with the broken trunk? Or the mug whose handle chipped off? These things seem to pile up quickly, and if you haven't fixed them yet, you probably aren't going to. Do yourself a favor, accept that they aren't going to get repaired, and get them out of your house.

Have a Donation Box

This is mentioned throughout this book, but it's a great idea to always have a donation box in your house. It encourages you to do something with the shirt or dress you see in your closet but never wear instead of just stuffing it aside and letting it continue to be useless and collect dust. Please take care to donate the box as soon as it's full. Getting rid of things quickly is the best way to ensure they won't sneak back into your cabinets, drawers, etc.

***

By implementing these habits, you're showing yourself and your family that you are serious and committed to keeping a clutter-free, organized home. Remember, decluttering is never one-and-done. It requires constant upkeep and daily effort. But you can do it!

Chapter Eight

Level Up!

> "Amidst all the clutter, beyond all the obstacles, aside from all the static, are the goals set. Put your head down, do the best job possible, let the flak pass, and work toward those goals."
>
> ~ Donald Rumsfeld

After each check-in you perform on yourself amidst your journey toward a neat and tidy lifestyle, you should almost always find a way in which you can improve, change, or adapt. Again, this is a life-long process, and we hope that this prospect is exciting to you. Life is a highway, baby! And you gotta learn to ride it—and love to continually ride it—until you take your last breath. Think about it this way: tomorrow, you have the chance to be an even better version of yourself than you were today.

Challenges and Setbacks

Let's face it, for as many steps forward that you take, you'll probably take just as many backward. That's just human nature. Our lives are never-ending rollercoasters of triumph and failure.

When it comes to decluttering in particular, the challenges and setbacks you face may be in the form of (or at least similar to) one or more of the following:

- Being exhausted from raising one or multiple small children and just leaving their toys out instead of doing your nightly routine of picking them up before bed

- You have to stay late at work, so the reorganization you planned to do of your closet that night will have to wait

- Falling ill and behind on your daily "chores" because you don't have the energy to do them

- Planning to do your laundry on a Sunday afternoon but deciding you could use a picnic with your best friend instead

- Rescuing a dog and focusing on potty training or establishing a bond and trust instead of the accumulating fur on your carpet

- Planning to go through your kitchen on a Saturday, but your sister calls and asks you to take your niece to her soccer tournament

One way or another, life gets in the way. And when it does, it's okay to acknowledge it, surrender to it, and then regroup later.

The most important thing is that you don't get frustrated and throw in the towel altogether. This is part of that life-long journey we already talked about. At points, keeping your house as organized and as clean as you'd like it to be is going to be tough. What will make or break you is how you react to those challenging times. If you are kind to yourself, do what you need to do in order to stay physically and mentally healthy (like doing dishes so they don't get moldy, cleaning animal excrement off the floor, keeping your bathroom in a livable condition, disposing of old food in your fridge, etc.), you're doing *enough*. Maybe that won't be enough tomorrow or the next day, but if it's enough for today, that's fine. Just don't abandon those goals altogether.

Another thing to consider is the fact that the cleaning and organizing "game" of doing little by little (like picking up a piece of lint when you see it on the floor or scraping crumbs off the counter after you make some toast) will become so good that a few days of neglect won't seem as noticeable or catastrophic.

The Importance of Meditation and Mindfulness Techniques

As we've said and hopefully demonstrated, when decluttering your space, it's just as important to focus on doing the same in your mind. Negative thoughts, false excuses, and anything else that is not supporting or benefiting you is all just clutter. It's covering up the beauty that's inside of you and the power you hold in your brain.

So, meditating, practicing hypnotherapy, or any other kind of mindful decluttering that you can undertake is key.

But just a quick hint: practicing mindfulness often requires unplugging (unless, of course, you're using your phone to listen to a video or audio recording) from a device and just focusing on (or "plugging into") yourself. If you fail to do this, you might miss out on all the wonderful things that meditation, hypnotherapy, and mindfulness in general have to offer!

Remember It's a Practice

As you're going through your mindfulness journey, please remember that it's not a standard of perfection or a set of ideals to hold yourself to. Instead, it's a practice, one that you will continually need to take time for, and that will not always be easy. However, if you stay with it, you'll find that your mind goes into a positive, mindful place by default. When it sneaks back into the negative, give yourself grace and do your best to reroute your thoughts.

Declutter Like a Pro

We've already given you countless tips for removing the unnecessary clutter from your house, but here are even more (yes, we have more, if you can believe it).

- **Take Almost Everything off Your Floor:** Besides furniture, floor lamps, minimal vases, rugs, and the occasional decorative little bin for pillows or blankets, your floor should be clear. Contrary to how some people treat the floors in their homes…it's not one giant storage bin (or it shouldn't be if you're looking to tidy up your life).

- **Designate a Spot for Junk:** Limit yourself to <u>one</u> small space—either in your kitchen, by your front door, etc., for the little bits and bobs (like bag clips, twisty ties, envelopes, pens, and batteries) that don't fit anywhere in your house. Make sure that you regularly sort your junk drawers out and discard items as necessary. "Junk" doesn't have to equate to clutter! And here's another thing to consider—using little muffin tins or small containers to "group" stuff together in that space can help make them easier to find.

- **Use Magnetic Desk Organizers:** By doing this, you can rest assured that your paperclips, magnets, binder clips, and bulletin board tacks are secure and available when you need them.

- **Pick a Donation Center or Resell Method Before You Start Decluttering:** For instance, you can choose to go with any number of the following choices.

    - Sell gently used clothes to a consignment shop—a place where second-hand clothing and other items are sold.

    - Hold a yard sale or garage sale. These can take a lot of work...so be prepared for that. If you don't want to go to the trouble, ask around and see if any or your neighbors are planning to hold one soon. You can always give your things to them to sell.

    - Donate food and gently used toys from your own pets that have passed to your local animal shelter.

    - Give items to a non-profit.

        - Dress for Success is a not-for-profit organization that empowers women in the workforce and in life by providing services, tools, and professional attire to secure employment and advance their careers. *How to donate*: Drop donations off at your nearest affiliate location (which can be found online). Each one has specific days and times when they are open and accepting donations, so make sure to call ahead of time.

        - The American Red Cross is one of the oldest and most-respected humanitarian organizations that provides emergency assistance, disaster relief, and disaster preparedness education for people around the world. They also partner with GreenDrop, which is an organization that sells donated items to thrift stores to benefit the Red Cross. *How to donate*: Find your nearest

GreenDrop drop-off center or schedule an at-home pick-up.

- Free the Girls accepts new and gently used bras in all styles and gives them to survivors of human trafficking in places like Uganda, El Salvador, and Mozambique to sell in second-hand markets and earn income for themselves and their families. *How to donate*: Fill out a donation form, which can be found on their website, and then find your nearest drop-off location. (You can only drop five bras off at a time).

- Goodwill is a well-known place to donate clothes, household items, etc., that uses its revenue to help people find employment through training, job placements, and other community-based programs. *How to donate*: Drop donations off at your local store and donation center.

- One Warm Coat is a non-profit that provides free coats to people in need. *How to donate*: Drop new or gently used coats to active coat drives (typically in the fall and winter months) or at one of their non-profit partners in your area (can be found online). However, like other organizations on this list, you should call first to check for drop-off hours.

- Planet Aid strives to divert textiles from landfills by accepting almost all used clothing that has holes, small stains, or tears and giving them to be sold and reused in developing countries. The only clothes that will not be accepted are wet, dirty beyond repair, or moldy. *How to donate*: Put all unwanted clothing into a bag and drop it off at one of the 19,000 drop-off locations across the country.

- The Salvation Army is an international charity that provides services to millions of Americans through their work in homeless shelters, conducting disaster relief, and providing support for veterans, the elderly, and members of the LGBTQ+ community. *How to donate*: Make a donation at a drop-off center near you or schedule a pick-up.

- Soles4Souls has the sole (pun intended) focus of turning shoes and clothing into opportunities for people in need. It accepts new or gently used shoes and clothing and gives them away to be worn or sold across the country. *How to donate*: Ship donations with Zappos for Good, which provides prepaid shipping labels for UPS, or you can find a drop-off location.

- Vietnam Veterans of America serves the needs of Vietnam Veterans by giving donated clothes, shoes, and household items to homeless or low-income veterans or selling them in their resale stores to raise funds for their programs and initiatives. *How to donate*: Find a drop-off location or schedule a pick-up.

- And many, many more! Check for resources around your town for more suggestions.

○ Sell your things online (But for goodness' sake, please be careful when meeting up with strangers. Always choose a public location with lots of other people around).

○ For those of you on the crafty side, you can turn old clothing into rugs or blankets.

- Donate to your local homeless shelters. (You can simply call them and ask if they're accepting donations at this time).

- Or you can just throw old items away or give them to your friends and family members.

- **Hang Kids' Artwork from Clips:** Your children likely enjoy having their masterpieces put on display in your kitchen, but they don't need to stay up there forever. Hanging them from magnetic clips can avoid clutter while also making it easier to change the pictures out and more interesting to look at than regular magnets.

- **Use Shower Curtain Rings:** to hold just about everything. Shower curtain rods and rings aren't only useful for your bathroom. They can be used in closets to hold up purses, scarves, and belts, and in the kitchen to hang dishtowels or rags on.

- **Clean up Entryways or Mudrooms with Built-In Storage, Bins, and Hooks:** Entryways and mudrooms are breeding grounds for clutter because they are the first place you go when you walk into your house. So, you likely dump all kinds of stuff there. Utilizing storage bins, installing hooks, and shelves can help. Take things like umbrellas, hats, gloves, etc., that you grab on the go off the floor and put them in easy-to-retrieve spots (like the hooks we already mentioned).

- **Be Prepared with Baskets:** Having decorative baskets (that do not detract from your decorating scheme) is a great way to declutter areas of your house. For instance, use one in the living room for all the chargers and remotes.

- **Create a Clutter Cabinet:** You can designate a "clutter cabinet" in your house to hold tchotchkes, seasonal décor, candlesticks, picnic supplies, and anything else you may not need all the time.

That way, they'll be away and out of sight but readily accessible when you do need them.

- **Have a System for Storing Magazine Clippings:** There's no reason we can think of for saving an entire magazine for just one recipe or picture you deem as "fashion inspo." Instead, you can organize some kind of filing system to sort and store different stray notes. For instance, perhaps you are really into knitting and find an article about a new pattern you want to try. You can rip it out and store it in the folder you label "Knitting."

- **Invest in a Shredder:** So many of us panic when we have documents we deem to have sensitive information about ourselves or someone in our family on it and just "store" them in random places around your house. This is a great way for paper clutter to accumulate, and a solution would be to get a paper shredder.

- **Save Countertop Space:** Do you have one of those knife blocks that take up huge chunks of your valuable counter space? Never fear! Instead, get a magnetic strip to hang on your wall for knives to stick to. Alternatively, you can also put them in drawers with dividers.

- **Use Storage-Friendly Furniture:** Almost any piece of furniture can double as a storage unit. Blankets can be stored in an ottoman, overflow clothes can go into the drawers of nightstands or on bookshelves, and you can always use the dead space under your bed.

- **Create Clutter Hub Spots throughout Your Home:** Having "hallway hubs" helps keep those spaces clear. Think of them like way stations to place items—like shoes, etc.—that would otherwise resemble clutter if they were just haphazardly strown about. With that in mind, you should be able to decipher the perfect locations in your house for them.

- **Treat Every Item in Your Home the Way You Treat a Fork:** If you start thinking of every item in your home as a fork, it will soon become obvious to you when something is out of place. If you found a fork in your bathroom, it would be obvious that it doesn't belong there. Instead, it goes in the drawer next to your sink—or wherever—with your other utensils. Every item in your house should have a specific, designated spot where it goes.

- **Use Your Smartphone:** For crying out loud! We're in the age of technology, so you might as well use the darn things! Taking pictures of paper menus and schedules is a great way to avoid paper clutter. Don't save paperwork you can easily find online, such as user manuals, credit card statements, and take-out menus.

- **Use Hanging Storage:** Hanging shoe organizers can be used for other like jewelry, gloves, scarves, boxed and canned food, and more! The clear pockets are handy because it's easy to see what's stored inside each one.

- **Store Plastic Bags for Later Use:** To help the environment, consider keeping the plastic shopping bags you've acquired for later use. They can be wastebasket liners and doggy bags. An expert hack is to keep them concealed in old paper towel tubes. You just have to crunch them together in small balls and stuff them inside.

- **Store Seasonally:** Rotate your seasonal items into the front of your closet so the clothing you're going to be wearing most often will be easily accessible to you. Plus, this will give you the chance to examine all your seasonal clothing when the weather starts to change. You can see if there's anything in your wardrobe that you no longer like, no longer need, or need to repair.

- **Use Baskets in the Linen Closet:** Like mudrooms, linen closets are prone to clutter. Putting bath towels and other things in designated baskets can help keep you nice and organized.

- **Give Everyone's Items a Space:** Especially if you have a large family, consider giving every member their own basket or shoe bin in the entryway, mudroom, or foyer. This is an excellent way of keeping everybody's belongings together and out of the way.

- **Frequently Declutter Your Purse or Backpack:** Every week, month, or whenever you feel it necessary, you should empty out your purses and backpacks. Many of us don't even realize it, but we're carrying around heavy garbage cans. To avoid that, dump everything out and throw out old pieces of gum, receipts, tissues, straw wrappers, old grocery lists, and anything else you no longer need while preserving the essentials (sunglasses, lip balm, your wallet, etc.).

- **Unsubscribe from Mailings You Don't Read:** As we covered in the digital clutter section, unread emails quickly become clutter, and the same is true for physical mail. A lot of us get magazines, catalogs, and newsletters that we never read and instead just toss out. If you're one of these people, please consider canceling your subscriptions. It's a waste of resources for it to be delivered to your home every month, week, etc.

- **Use a Scanner for Office Clutter:** Scanning documents and saving them electronically is a great way to get rid of paper clutter, and it's arguably a safer method for storing sensitive and important documents—like taxes, mortgages, warranties, etc.

Declutter for the Holidays: While preparing to decorate for the holidays, set aside some decorations (ornaments, pillows, lights, etc.) and then donate them to have a clutter-free Christmas. Moreover, you may want to inventory wrapping paper, bows, boxes, and ribbon that you already have before buying more. After that, either give them to someone who will use them or use them up yourself.

- Plus, you may want to rethink the gifts you give to people. Ask, "Will this add clutter to their life?" If yes, perhaps another choice would be better for that person. (Unless they specifically asked for it.)

- However, asking for assistance shouldn't be a *common* occurrence. Otherwise, you risk using people. Instead, you should reserve reaching out in desperate times (like when you have a newborn baby, are dealing with an illness or injury, etc.).

Don't Add Clutter to Your Home or Others

We've been covering how to declutter your home, but it's equally important for you not to "leave a trace" behind at other peoples' houses either. Wherever you go, be careful to pick up after yourself. Never leave a place dirtier or worse for wear after you leave. It's just rude! Plus, you're communicating to others how you expect them to act when in your home. If you trash their place, they will have the incentive (and unspoken consent) to act the same way among your things.

***

Please take the time to sit with each of these suggestions and consider integrating them into your life. It will only improve for it.

Chapter Nine

Simple Doesn't Mean Basic

> "When we clear the physical clutter from our lives, we literally make way for inspiration and 'good, orderly direction' to enter."
>
> ~ Julia Cameron

Fortunately, being simple (and minimal) doesn't mean you have to be boring or like anyone else. In fact, that couldn't be further from the truth. By eliminating the extraneous "stuff" in your life, you'll get a better understanding of yourself and the things that you value and need.

For example, let's pretend that you are going through a drawer of an old nightstand that's been sitting in your parents' basement for years. You find a letter, and it's from your deceased grandmother whom you miss dearly. Something tells you that this is something you need to keep. That feeling informs you just how much your grandma meant to you, and it shows that you are a sentimental person. Of course, if you don't have those feelings, that's totally fine and normal for you too.

Life's Crucial Nuances

To find balance, you must first understand the subtle differences that exist in this world—especially in terms of organizing, cleaning, and decluttering. It's important to understand these slight differences to understand what living up to your highest potential looks like.

Plentiful Stuff vs. True Abundance

Having plenty of things—clothes to wear, cookware to prepare meals on, blankets to keep warm, etc.—is simply having *stuff*. That doesn't necessarily equate to your wealth, status in life, or mental well-being. True abundance refers to having every desire and need met at the same time. So, to know true abundance is to know joy, happiness, purpose, love, and vitality at once. And for most, that requires having just enough without worrying about going into scarcity, feeling selfish, or like there are piles of things in your home that you don't use and cause you anxiety. So often, we get these two concepts mixed up or confused with one another.

Having Enough vs. Hoarding

Ideally, you should strive to have the ideal number (which is different for everyone) of things to support you in having a comfortable, healthy, and enjoyable lifestyle. What you want to avoid is having too many—or seeking out physical items to provide you with the solution to your sadness or depression.

An example of the difference would be a mother (woman A) of several children who makes a six-figure salary and loves to bake cookies every holiday season. So, she needs several baking sheets, cooking sprays, pounds of flour, chocolate chips, frosting, sprinkles, etc. These are things she personally needs to feel happy and fulfilled. On the other side, a single, unemployed college student (woman B) who doesn't like sweets or baking would have no use for such things, and they'd likely go bad in her possession instead of being joyfully consumed.

Woman A is working from her means and using her money to purchase and do the things she and her family enjoy. If woman B did the same thing, she would be risking going into debt by purchasing the supplies with money on credit cards (i.e., money she doesn't have), and it would all be for nothing. In fact, she could be hoarding the stuff from woman A, who gets so much good out of it.

Another example would be a wealthy fashion model who has a ginormous apartment with a walk-in closet. Through his work and lifestyle, he's acquired a lot of clothes. But he's worked out a healthy rotation between them when going out to highly photographed events. Within reason, this could be healthy for him. He can afford them, and he has enough appreciation for each item that he works them into recurring outfits.

At the opposite end is a man who is unhappy in his marriage because he feels like his wife is no longer sexually attracted to him based on the weight he's recently gained. Instead of dedicating himself to working out, he buys a bunch of clothing he thinks will make him feel better about himself (and more attractive to his wife). But in his heart of hearts, he knows he won't feel good in them, and therefore doesn't wear them. So, his closet is just getting full of useless junk.

Man A is living his best life while man B is wasting it and putting a dirty bandage on an open wound instead of going to a doctor to have it taken care of.

"Good Enough" vs. Done Correctly

Especially when cleaning or organizing, so many of us have this bad habit of exerting "just enough" effort—like wiping down a bookshelf without taking everything down and getting the whole thing clean—but this behavior doesn't make us feel good or like we accomplished something. Instead, we often feel bad about ourselves for not fully going the extra mile. In order to transform our homes and our minds, we must fully commit. Again, that doesn't require perfection. It requires persistence.

How to Declutter and Still Be Unique

This has already been touched on a bit, but the answer is pretty simple: feel the freedom to hold onto the things that spark joy for you. This will leave you with the feeling of having a space that you're comfortable in and that speaks to you. That's also a good way to motivate yourself to eliminate clutter. By holding onto it, you're communicating to yourself and others that you identify with it and that it reflects who you are on the inside. If you're like most, you probably don't want a bunch of mess to represent you. Instead, you likely want to get rid of anything that is an eyesore, is never used, or has already served its purpose, and focus on your minimal, prized possessions and those that help you ascend to your highest potential.

If you feel like you could benefit from different methodologies when decluttering your home, below are a few that you can try.

20/20 Rule

So many of us hold onto things we don't need "just in case." But this rule suggests you get rid of (by throwing away, donating, giving away, or selling) anything that you can replace for $20 or less and in twenty minutes' time.

Pros: You will get rid of a ton of stuff by the end of this exercise—things like creams, tchotchkes, over-the-counter medications, and other little things you have around the house.

Cons: There may come a time when you actually need those items, and instead of finding them in your cabinet or drawer, you're going to have to go out and repurchase them.

Traveler's Method

Pretend like you're planning for a trip, and declutter your house the same way you'd pack a suitcase. Designating one caddy for toiletries, for example, fill it up with the necessities and then throw away, sell, or give away the rest.

Minimalist Game

Beginning the first day of the month, the number of things you purge corresponds to the day that day. So, on day one, you donate one thing, on day two, you donate two, and so on and so forth. At the end of the month, you'll end up removing almost five hundred items from your home.

Pros: It's an effective way of decluttering your home or office.

Cons: It takes a significant commitment to complete this challenge.

Project 333: The Minimalist Fashion Challenge

This method relies on the constraint that you can only wear thirty-three articles of clothing for the next few months. Clothing, accessories, jewelry, coats, and shoes count toward that number (exceptions include wedding rings, underwear, sleepwear, in-home loungewear, and workout clothes). Everything else should be packed away and hidden.

Chances are you'll find that even with a closet full of clothes, you are constantly pulling out the same pieces over and over, and this challenge will help you see what your favorites and essentials are.

Pros: It's an effective way of showing you how to rely on a select number of pieces in your closet.

Cons: There come times when you have to wear something out of the ordinary—like a dress to a fancy wedding, a suit coat to an interview, etc. So, this experiment doesn't always work.

Swedish Death Cleaning

Don't worry, this isn't as sinister or scary as it seems. Instead, it's a frame of mind to get into. As you work to declutter your home, think about eliminating the things that are unnecessary to take the burden off your family members later when you pass. It is all about holding onto essential belongings and purging all the rest.

- Examine clothing, shoes, and accessories.
    - Sort through clothing.
    - See what still fits.
    - Make a "toss" pile

- Get your closet in order.
- Go through furniture and other items.
  - Start with items that take up the most space.
  - Work your way down to smaller items.
  - Decide what to keep and what to discard.
  - Make a dedicated pile of mementos.
- Address digital clutter.
  - Gather login credentials for loved ones.
  - Declutter desktops and laptops.
  - Declutter hard drives.
  - Keep up with your email.
- Gather important paperwork.
  - Designate an area for important files.
  - Make sure loved ones know where to look.
  - If you have a will, make sure it's up to date.
- Sort with intention.
  - Make a "Donate" pile.
  - Make a "Sell" pile.
  - Make a "Keepsakes/Mementos" pile.

- Make a "Discard" pile.

Discuss your reasoning and methodology with your family and loved ones. They might think it's strange, especially if you're healthy, but you can explain to them that this is merely a way for you to minimize your home—the added bonus that your affairs are also getting sorted is just the cherry on top!

Pros: At the end, you're going to feel very accomplished and prepared for the worst.

Cons: It can be quite depressing thinking about your demise and the aftermath of your family having to deal with your things.

Packing Party

This is a more extreme decluttering technique, and it requires you to invite a bunch of friends over and pretend like you're packing to move (it's even better if you actually are moving). Then, going forward, you only take out the items that you need. After three months, whatever is left in the box can be thrown away, recycled, given away, sold, or donated.

Pros: You'll walk away from this exercise with a better understanding of the things in your home that you use and need consistently.

Cons: It might seem foolish to engage in this challenge if you aren't actually packing up and moving to a new apartment or house.

Closet Hanger Method

As per the name, this technique only works for clothes you keep on a hanger. But to start, you want to make sure that all your hangers are facing the same way. Then, each day when you place whatever you wore back into your closet, put the hangers facing the opposite way of the rest. Within a month or two, you'll have a better idea of the clothes you actually wear.

Pros: This is a great way for you to take notice of the things in your closet that you reach for most often.

Cons: It doesn't work well with your other clothes like those in your dresser, etc.

KonMari Method

Instead of deciding what to get rid of, this method focuses on what to *keep*. And you deem that based on whether or not a particular item sparks joy in you when you hold or look at it.

Pros: You'll have the opportunity to comprehend which of your possessions truly make you happy.

Cons: This is another time-consuming method. It doesn't just focus on one area of your home like a closet or dresser. Instead, you have to go through every single belonging.

Four-Box Method

Set up four boxes, as the name suggests, and label them: "Put away," "Give away," "Throw away," and "Undecided." Then, as you go through your things, place them into the corresponding box.

Pro: It's straightforward and gives you the opportunity to put things in the "Undecided" box, for you to decide about at a later time.

Con: It starts to get tricky when you have too many things in the "Undecided" box. In that case, you're basically giving yourself another massive chore. So, you should probably avoid putting things in there as much as possible.

One Method

Similar to other exercises we've covered, this one requires that you get rid of one thing every single day—be that one item, one box of things, or one bag.

Pro: This will make decluttering part of your daily routine.

Con: It can be hard to keep up in the midst of busy schedules or traveling. Also, it isn't ideal for people who prefer to go on "pitch" frenzies and purge a lot in a short amount of time.

The 90/90 Rule

If you're looking to declutter, an easy way is to go through your belongings and ask yourself two questions—"Have I used this in the last ninety days?" and "Will I use this in the next ninety days?" If the answer to both is no, you may want to consider getting rid of that item.

Pros: It helps you recognize the things in your home that you no longer use or need.

Cons: It doesn't work well for seasonal or sentimental items.

Decluttering Checklist

Not sure where to start your decluttering process? No worries! You can either follow printable templates online or make your own.

An example might look like this:

Go Through All Toys	Clean Out Holiday Décor	Clean out Spare Bathroom	Go Through the Kids' Clothes	Sort All Electronics
Clean Out Utensil Drawer	Go Through Spice Cabinet	Clean Out Fridge	Clean Out Pantry	Go Through Dishes and Tupperware
Go Through Baking Supplies	Empty the Junk Drawer	Clean Out Office/Desks	Go Through Art Supplies/Craft Room	Go Through DVDs
Go Through Cleaning Supplies	Donate Clothes You Never Wear	Clean Out Car	Go Through Nightstands	Sort Through Linen Closet
Clean Out Purse	Go Through All Makeup	Go Through Medicine Cabinet	Match All Socks and Throw Away Singles	Clean Basement

If you want to make your own, sit down and decipher how many days you think you want to do the challenge (one task per day), and then decipher the areas in your home that could use some organizing. Then cross off each square as you go along. This is beneficial because you'll have to identify the places in your house that would benefit from a bit of tidying, and you'll get the satisfaction of crossing each task off when you're done. At the end, you'll have a completely crossed-out piece of paper—imagine how good that will feel!

Pros: Exactly what we already mentioned with the awareness and sense of accomplishment.

Cons: Some people think too big, and make their checklists really long. Then they become discouraged and either start and fall off the process or don't do it at all.

Five-Item Rule

Go into every room of your house and decide to get rid of five (at a minimum—you can always choose more) items in each one.

Pro: This is a low-stress way to start decluttering.

Con: With the expectation of only getting rid of five things in each room, you may feel like you haven't accomplished much by the end of it.

***

No matter what rule, method, technique, or mixture of them you pick, you must decide early on that you're going to stick to it. If you do, you'll see results in no time!

Conclusion

Dear reader,

As we reach the end of our shared journey through the pages of this book, it's time to reflect on the path you're about to embark upon. The decision before you isn't just a choice; it's a commitment. A commitment to break free from the clutter that's been holding you back, both physically and mentally.

Think about the clutter in your life. It's not just about the items that fill up your closets and drawers. It's about the *mental* clutter, the emotional baggage, the things that weigh down your spirit and cloud your mind. Decluttering isn't just about creating space in your home; it's about creating space in your soul for peace—for joy.

Imagine a life where every item in your home brings you satisfaction or serves a purpose. Imagine a life where you're not constantly burdened by the things you don't need or don't use. This is the life that awaits you on the other side of decluttering. It's a life of simplicity, a life of clarity, a life where *you* maintain control.

As you stand on the threshold of this new chapter, remember that decluttering is a journey, not a destination. It's a process that requires patience, commitment, and a willingness to let go. But the rewards are immeasurable. With each item you discard, with each space you clear, you'll feel lighter, freer, and more at peace.

But where do you start? Start with one item, one drawer, one room. Start with what feels manageable. And as you start to see the changes—as you start to *feel* the difference—you'll be motivated to keep going. Before you know it, you'll have transformed not just your space but your entire outlook on life.

Throughout this journey, be gentle with yourself. There will be moments of frustration, moments of doubt. But there will also be moments of profound bliss. Embrace the process, embrace the change, and most importantly, embrace the new you that will emerge.

As you venture forth, remember that decluttering isn't a solitary journey. Reach out to friends, family, or online communities for support and inspiration. Share your successes, no matter how small. Celebrate your progress, and learn from your setbacks. You're not alone in this.

And as you declutter your physical space, take the time to declutter your spirit as well. Practice mindfulness and/or meditation—or simply take a few moments each day to sit in silence and reflect. You'll be amazed at how much mental clutter you can clear by simply giving yourself the space and time to breathe.

As you move forward, keep in mind that decluttering is an ongoing process. It's about making conscious choices about what you bring into your life and what you let go of. It's about living intentionally, living mindfully, and living in a way that brings you joy and peace.

We hope that this book has been a valuable guide. We hope that it has inspired you, motivated you, and equipped you with the tools you need to transform your space and your life. Remember, you deserve clarity, simplicity, and fulfillment. And it all starts with decluttering.

So, dear reader, as you turn the final page of this book, remember that this isn't the end. It's just the beginning. The beginning of a new way of living—a new way of being. A life unburdened by clutter, a life filled with purpose and peace.

Thank you for joining us on this journey. Thank you for choosing to make a change. And thank you for believing in the power of decluttering to transform your life!

With heartfelt gratitude and best wishes for your continued journey,

Deborah LeBlanc

Additional Resources

Books

Clutterfree with Kids, by Joshua Becker (2014)

- From the Amazon description: "Children add joy, purpose, and meaning to our lives. They provide optimism, hope, and love. They bring smiles, laughter, and energy into our homes. They also add clutter. As parents, balancing life and managing clutter may appear impossible—or at the very least, never-ending. But what if there was a better way to live? *Clutterfree with Kids* offers a new perspective and fresh approach to overcoming clutter."

Cozy Minimalist Home: More Style, Less Stuff, by Myquillyn Smith (2018)

- From the Amazon description: "Go beyond décor trends to make your home beautiful, stylish, and comfortable . . . *on any budget.* Writing for the hands-on woman who'd rather move her own furniture before hiring a designer, Myquillyn Smith—author of *The Nesting Place*—helps you think through every room in your house, one purposeful design at a time."

Digital Minimalism: Choosing a Focused Life in a Noisy World, by Cal Newport (2019)

- From the Amazon description: "Drawing on a diverse array of real-life examples, from Amish farmers to harried parents to Silicon Valley programmers, Newport identifies the common practices of digital minimalists and the ideas that underpin them. He shows how digital minimalists are rethinking their relationship to social media, rediscovering the pleasure of the offline world, and reconnecting with their inner selves through regular periods of inner solitude."

Everything That Remains: A Memoir by The Minimalists, by Joshua Fields Millburn and Ryan Nicodemus (2014)

- From the Amazon description: "Not a how-to book but a why-to book, *Everything That Remains* is the touching, surprising story of what happened when one young man decided to let go of everything and begin living deliberately."

Goodbye, Things: The New Japanese Minimalism, by Fumio Sasaki (2017)

- From the Amazon description: "Sasaki modestly shares his personal minimalist experience, offering specific tips on the minimizing process and revealing how the minimalist movement can not only transform your space but truly enrich your life."

Hello, Habits: A Minimalist's Guide, by Fumio Sasaki (2021)

- From the Amazon description: "Sasaki explains how we can acquire the new habits that we want—and get rid of the ones that do us any good. Drawing on leading theories and tips about the science of habit formation from cognitive psychology, neuroscience, and sociology, along with examples from popular culture and tried-and-tested techniques from his own life, he unravels common misconceptions about 'willpower' and 'talent,' and offers a step-by-step guide to success."

Home in Harmony: Designing an Inspiring Life, by Christa O'Leary (2014)

- From the Amazon description: "We all deserve a calm, well-ordered, pleasantly designed refuge where we can relax and enjoy our families. Having had four children in a little more than five years while running a thriving design business, with the body of a fit runner who does yoga and meditates, Christa O'Leary has become the guardian at the gate of our sanctuaries—our homes. She teaches us to be aware of the toxins found in both our food and furnishings; the detrimental effects of our unhealthy habits; and society's frantic need to have the latest gadgets, to get ahead, and to be forever on the go."

L'art de la Simplicite: How to Live More with Less, by Dominique Loreau (translated by Louise Lalaurie) (2017)

- From the Amazon description: "Living in Japan and inspired by Asian philosophy, Loreau takes you on a step-by-step journey to a clutter-free home, a calm mind and an energized body. Free yourself of possessions you don't want or need; have more money to spend on life's little luxuries; eat better and lose weight; and say goodbye to anxiety and negative relationships."

Love People, Use Things: Because the Opposite Never Works, by Joshua Fields Millburn and Ryan Nicodemus (2021)

- From the Amazon description: "Imagine a life with less: less stuff, less clutter, less stress and debt and discontent—a life with fewer distractions. Now, imagine a life with more: more meaningful relationships, more growth and contribution and contentment—a life of passion, encumbered by the trappings of the chaotic world around you."

Make Sh** Happen! How to Unleash REAL Power Into Your Life, by Deborah LeBlanc (2024)

- Deborah LeBlanc's Make Sh** Happen is a call to action for dreamers stuck in neutral. Consider this book the first stepping stone on your pathway toward true accomplishment. Inside, you'll discover a treasure trove of wisdom, from myth-busting science to productivity hacks that make progress feel like playtime. You'll map your trajectory by way of insightful exercises, then watch your efficiency soar—at last. With witty warmth and cold hard facts, this little book will make a big difference, facilitating a mindset shift that's guaranteed to take you off the sofa and test your limits. The outcome? A life you've only imagined—a life you've never dared to claim. It's time to cut through the nasty habits, endless excuses, and sloppy plans. It's time to work smart instead of hard. It's time to make sh** happen!

Miss Minimalist: Inspiration to Downsize, Declutter, and Simplify, by Francine Jay (2011)

- From the Amazon description: "Along with valuable tips and advice the author shares her personal stories about decluttering and living with less."

Outer Order, Inner Calm: Declutter & Organize to Make More Room for Happiness, by Gretchen Rubin (2020)

- From the Amazon description: "Ask yourself DO I NEED IT? DO I LOVE IT? DO I USE IT? With 150 concrete clutter-clearing ideas, insights, strategies, and sometimes surprising tips, Gretchen tackles the key challenges of creating outer order by explaining how to 'make choices,' 'create order,' 'know yourself;' 'cultivate useful habits,' and of course, how to 'add beauty.'"

Stuffocation: Why We've Had Enough of Stuff and Need Experience More Than Ever, by James Wallman (2015)

- From the Amazon description: "Trend forecaster James Wallman traces our obsession with stuff back to the original *Mad Men*, who first created desire through advertising. He interviews anthropologists studying the clutter crisis, economists searching for new ways of measuring profess, and psychologists who link stuffocation to declining well-being."

The Life-Changing Magic of Tidying Up: The Japanese Art of Decluttering and Organizing, by Marie Kondo (2014)

- From the Amazon description: "With detailed guidance for determining which items in your house 'spark joy' (and which don't), this international bestseller will help you clear your clutter and enjoy the unique magic of a tidy home—and the calm, motivated mindset it can inspire."

The Minimalist Way: Minimalism Strategies to Declutter Your Life and Make Room for Joy, by Erica Layne (2019)

- From the Amazon description: "Discover how to apply the minimalist to every aspect of your life by changing the way you think about your home, career, relationships, and money. *The Minimalist Way* will help you take one step at a time with simple exercises and activities. Ease into minimalism at your own pace and learn how to let go."

The More of Less: Finding the Life You Want Under Everything You Own, by Joshua Becker (2016)

- From the Amazon description: "While excess consumption leads to bigger houses, faster cars, fancier technology, and cluttered homes, it never brings happiness. Rather, it results in a desire for more. It redirects our greatest passions to things that can never fulfill, and it distracts us from the very lives we wish we were living. But it doesn't have to be that way…It's time to own your possessions instead of letting them own you. After all, the beauty of minimalism isn't what it takes away. It's in what it gives."

The Neuroscience of Mindfulness: The Astonishing Science Behind How Everyday Hobbies Help You Relax, by Stan Rodski (2019)

- From the Amazon description: "Explore the benefits of a mindful approach to life. Cutting-edge studies in neuroscience have in recent years proved what many doctors, therapists, and other health professionals have long suspected: simple, repetitive tasks, performed with focus and attention—mindfulness, in other words—can not only quieten our noisy thought processes and help us relax but also improve our outlook on life and protect us against a range of life-threatening illnesses."

The Power of Awareness: Unlocking the Law of Attraction, by Neville Goddard (1952)

- From the Amazon description: "Venturing into the realms of mysticism and religion, Neville's work is rooted in an empowering insistence on the agency of individuals to shape their own reality."

Things That Matter: Overcoming Distraction to Pursue a More Meaningful Life, by Joshua Becker (2022)

- From the Amazon description: "In *Things That Matter*, Joshua Becker uses practical exercises, questions, insights from a nationwide survey, and success stories to give you the motivation you need to: identify pursuits that matter most to you, align your dreams with your daily priorities, recognize how money and possessions keep you from happiness, become aware of how others' opinions of you influence your choices, embrace what you're truly passionate about instead of planning that next escape, figure out what to do with all those emails, notifications, and pings, and let go of past mistakes and debilitating habits."

Wherever You Go, There You Are: Mindfulness Meditation in Everyday Life, by Jon Kabat-Zinn (1994)

- From the Amazon description: "Find quiet reflective moments in your life—and reduce your stress levels drastically."

You Can Buy Happiness (and It's Cheap): How One Woman Radically Simplified Her Life and How You Can Too, by Tammy Strobel (2012)

- From the Amazon description: "In this book Strobel combines research on well-being with numerous real-world examples to offer practical inspiration. Her fresh take on our things, our work, and our relationships spells out micro-actions that anyone can take to step into a life that's more conscious and connected, sustainable and sustaining, heartfelt and *happy*."

Websites

ABowlFullOfLemons.com

- A place to find blog posts with tips and tricks to help you stay diligently organized, on a budget, and clean.

BecomingMinimalist.com

- A website with posts written by Joshua Becker about becoming and staying a minimalist.

ClutterFreeNow.com

- You can find videos and blog posts and book a free consultation with Pam Holland, a productivity, organizing, and life transformation coach, speaker, and teacher.

FreeMindfulness.org

- A place to get free downloadable mindfulness meditation exercises.

Mindful.org

- Find blog posts, guided meditations, and podcasts about having (and maintaining) a healthy mind and a healthy life.

MindPathTherapies.com

- The author of the *Make Sh** Happen* series' website. It provides resources on what hypnosis is and is not, various information on workshops she is offering, guided hypnotherapy audios, the opportunity to book her for one-on-one sessions, and more!

- Hypnotherapies can be purchased to address the following topics:

  - Anxiety Release

  - Assertiveness

  - Brain Power

  - Creativity

  - Deep Relaxation

  - Exercise Motivation

  - Guilt Release

  - Increase Self-Esteem

  - Insecurity

  - Motivation

  - Overcoming Shame

  - Performance Anxiety

  - Powerful Public Speaking

  - Problem-Solving

  - Stress Release

  - Worrying

Unclutterer.com

- Find expert cleaning advice from professionals.

ZenHabits.net

- A website about "finding the simplicity and mindfulness in the daily chaos of our lives," led by Leo Babauta, a father, author, and simplicity coach.

Podcasts Featuring Deborah LeBlanc

Buision – "Writing and Selling Books in Today's Age (With Deborah LeBlanc)" (Season 1, Episode 2).

Happily Ever Habits (January 25, 2022).

I Never Knew (INK) But My Dog Did! with Lifecoach Maureen – "Loss, Love, and Paranormal Entities" (Episode 32).

Life's Multiverse – "Rising from the Ashes with Deborah LeBlanc: On Resilience and Self-Limiting Beliefs" (December 8, 2023).

Resilient Minds 365 – "Deborah LeBlanc, Clinical Depression and Hypnotherapy" (Episode 57).

The Day After with CJ & Ashley – "Bringing Color Back into the World w/ Deborah LeBlanc" (Episode 17).

The Flare Up Show – "Letting Go of Limiting Beliefs" (Episode 62).

The Story Behind the Story with Matteo and Renata (Episode 60).

Trauma Unbroken Podcast with Michael Unbroken – "How To Find Yourself with Deborah LeBlanc" (Episode 249).

Other Podcasts

10% Happier with Dan Harris

- Dan Harris is a journalist who experienced the benefits of mindfulness and meditation in treating his anxiety.

A Slob Comes Clean

- Nony (Dana K White) from ASlobComesClean.com shares reality-based cleaning and organizing tips she learned through her own decluttering process.

An Uncluttered Life

- For tips and tricks to get the mess in your house under control and a dive into the potential reasons you let it get that unmanaged in the first place.

ClutterBug Podcast

- Tips and tricks to organize your home in just fifteen minutes a day.

Got Clutter? Get Organized!

- Janet M. Taylor is a professional organizer and brings guests on to discuss eliminating junk and creating the business and life that you want.

Mindfulness Mode

- An interview-based podcast about the scientific and practical aspects of mindfulness.

On Being

- Hosted by Krista Tippett and created as a digital gathering place for anyone interested in mindfulness.

One Organized Mama

- For organization and time management tips that are interesting, inspiring, and real.

Organize 365 Podcast

- For organization tips, strategies, and motivation with professional organizer Lisa Woodruff.

The Maximized Minimalist with Katy Jo Wells.

- Katy Wells is a decluttering expert who is passionate about helping moms get more joy out of life.

The Minimalists Podcast

- Netflix stars and best-selling authors Joshua Fields Millburn and Ryan Nicodemus discuss living with less stuff.

Untangle: Mindfulness for Curious Humans

- Hosted by former social media executives who are known for developing a headband that helps improve the quality of meditation sessions.

About the Author

Deborah LeBlanc is a Certified Clinical Hypnotherapist with certifications in ten other healing modalities that span over seventy presenting issues. Her expertise in relationship building has afforded her the opportunity to travel throughout the country as a keynote speaker and workshop facilitator.

www.ingramcontent.com/pod-product-compliance
Lightning Source LLC
Chambersburg PA
CBHW070115080526
44586CB00013B/1302